Luther for Armchair Theologians

Also available
in the Armchair Series:

Luther for Armchair Theologians

STEVEN PAULSON

ILLUSTRATIONS BY RON HILL

WJK WESTMINSTER
JOHN KNOX PRESS
LOUISVILLE · KENTUCKY

Scripture quotations from the New Revised Standard Version of the
Bible are copyright © 1989 by the Division of Christian Education
of the National Council of the Churches of Christ in the U.S.A.
and are used by permission.

Book design by Sharon Adams
Cover design by Jennifer K. Cox
Cover illustration: Ron Hill

First edition
Published by Westminster John Knox Press
Louisville, Kentucky

This book is printed on acid-free paper that meets the American
National Standards Institute Z39.48 standard. ∞

PRINTED IN THE UNITED STATES OF AMERICA

06 07 08 09 10 11 12 13 — 10 9 8 7 6 5 4 3

Library of Congress Cataloging-in-Publication Data

Paulson, Steven D.
    Luther for armchair theologians / Steven Paulson ; illustrated
by Ron Hill. — 1st ed.
        p. cm.
    Includes bibliographical references and index.
    ISBN-13: 978-0-664-22381-6 (alk. paper)
    ISBN-10: 0-664-22381-8 (alk. paper)
    1. Luther, Martin, 1483-1546. I. Title.

BR325.P35 2004
230'.41'092—dc22
                                        2004043039

No watcher waits with greater hope
than I for his returning.
—from Luther's hymn
"Out of the Depths"

Contents

INTRODUCTION

Let the reader beware! Luther has repeatedly proven to be as revolutionary as Copernicus and even more controversial. Luther understood himself to have been violently interrupted in his plan of steady progress toward heaven by God coming down to wrestle with him, even unto death. The wrestling took the form of the question, Where do I find a gracious God? Luther's question scorned what he called idle speculation, as if one had all the time in the world to get the answer and inquiring was no more perilous than reading a good book. When Luther stopped accepting the false answers of people around him, what he actually heard from God was breathtaking, especially since the church itself had repeatedly falsified the truth by substituting its own story for Christ's.

God, Luther found, did not want works, accomplishments, or justifications for why you practice your idiosyncratic, self-chosen religious or antireligious nonsense. God, who is right in himself (being God), has determined not only to be a God by himself but to be *your* God by directly addressing you *with words*—and not just any words either, but specific commands and promises that God is determined to have you hear. And when God is determined it is a holy sight to behold, whether it involves Abraham, Mary, Peter, Luther, or you. It frightens to death those who have made their own religion, just as it frightened Luther that his carefully practiced Christian religion was taken from him by God in what felt like a grand act of divine theft. Yet what first appeared as great loss of direction and mooring in such a great tradition as Latin Christianity soon became his opening unto life eternal by the resurrection from the dead. The Father of Jesus Christ sent his Son to die for sinners, including Luther, that their distrust might end and they be created anew as forgiven sinners by the Holy Spirit.

Luther's Story

On Thursday, the eighteenth of April, 1521, the "Luther Affair" burst on the world stage in a most public way. On that day Luther, an apparently inconsequential German monk, stood on trial before the whole church and empire. The two great powers of this world demanded he recant all his writings because they blasphemed God. Luther considered his fate before humans (he didn't want to disappoint his parents or be burned at the stake) and before God (he didn't want to blaspheme) in light of the repeated charge against his theology: "Are you the only one who knows?"

But Luther knew his was much more than a case of an individual conscience trying to express itself to powers that suppress individuality. That hour of his public trial had become, Luther thought, a crucial moment in the great struggle between God and the devil, and no one was more surprised than the obscure Augustinian hermit himself. There at Worms he finally uttered his famous confession:

> Unless I am convinced by the testimony of the Scriptures or by clear reason (for I do not trust either in the pope or in councils alone, since it is well known that they have often erred and contradicted themselves), I am bound by the Scriptures I have quoted and my conscience is captive to the Word of God. I cannot and I will not retract anything, since it is neither safe nor right to go against conscience. May God help me. Amen.[1]

"*Bound* by the Scriptures" with a conscience "*captive* to the Word of God" hardly sounds like freedom. But Scripture's freedom has never been an isolated, individualistic, lonely, and ultimately death-dealing notion like the ones that capture our imaginations today. True freedom is being captivated by Christ's promise of forgiveness of sins. It is like getting a tune in your head you can't get rid of, only this time instead of a legal refrain, "Have you done enough?" it repeats a promise: "God is pleased with you, on account of Christ." How did Luther come to be bound and captive to God's word this way?

Luther was born a peasant on November 10, 1483. On the Feast of St. Martin, his father took the boy to the church in Eisleben, Germany, to be baptized and named for the day's saint. Martin's family soon moved to Mansfeld, where his father began working in a copper mine. Though the Renaissance was blossoming at the great courts of Europe, daily life for the Luthers was a struggle to keep solvent, alive, and to have reasonable prospects for eternal life. Then, as now, the church imparted a basic kind of "spiritual" rule: "Do your best; God will do the rest." One of the notable theologians of the age, Gabriel Biel,

liked to use the Latin adage *facere quod in se est*, "to do what is within one," which God then accepts as "enough" out of kindness. Nowhere was that clearer than in the requirement to go to confession before a priest at least once a year. The priest would assess a penalty that could include such duties as prayers to saints or pilgrimages to holy sites with their "relics" (bones and such of departed saints).

But the center of religious life for the Luthers was the mass that would be offered to God as a sacrifice for sin by a properly ordained priest in fellowship with his bishop and the pope. The papal office that authorized a true mass was understood to extend back in time to Peter, the first among the disciples, and so to Christ himself. The Mass's form of sacrifice was a prayer built up over time around Jesus' last words to his disciples that offered up the cup of wine and the bread in a way that pleased God. For a long time this act had become so holy and separate from sinners that fears of misuse kept priests from giving the cup to those gathered in the church. So also the practice arose of "visual commun-ion," mystical participation in Christ's sacrificial suffering by the assembled faithful, who gazed at the altar bread as it was elevated by the priest during the long consecration prayer, the Mass canon. Even the act of a priest saying mass pri-vately, with no one listening or partaking of the body and blood, was taught as deliverance from sin—both in this life and beyond in what had become known as "purgatory." Purgatory was believed to be a place where souls not yet righteous or condemned would go to climb the great mountain of obedience and rid themselves of sin. Over all such church practices stood the office of the pope as head of all Christendom. The pope was able to allow tremendous variety of religious life, including reforming movements and religious groups of many kinds, as long as they remained loyal to his authority as the vicar (stand-in) of Christ on earth and Lord of the church—by divine right, as it was called. "Divine right" meant the office was believed to have been established by God's own demand and was God's means of extending law to new situations as they arose in history. Teachings could vary, even regarding the meaning of the Mass; loyalty to the pope could not.

The Religious Life and a New Discovery

Perhaps the most obvious presence of the church to most people in Luther's day, however, was the tremendous growth of monastic communities. Luther later thought that if monasteries kept to teaching, especially for the poor, they could serve a good purpose, but they had disastrously become a "better form" of the religious life than the every-day callings of Christians to be fathers, mothers, lawyers, doctors, and so on. He himself came into frequent contact with religious communities throughout his schooling, which eventually led him to the University of Erfurt. By 1505 he advanced to the master of arts degree and took up law. But he began to have other thoughts. While walking back to school from visiting his parents, he was caught in a thunderstorm, and in his fear Luther vowed to St. Anne, the patron saint of miners, to become a monk. His father was at first angry, then came around to the sense that this was indeed a divine sacrifice.

Luther gave away all he had and entered the Black Cloister of the Observant Augustinian Order in Erfurt, becoming a religious beggar—and a very good one at that. Luther frequently observed, "If anyone could have gained heaven as a monk, then I would indeed have been among them." But he would soon enough (1537, in the *Smalcald Articles*) call all that religious practice nothing but "human invention . . . not commanded, not necessary, not useful—while causing dangerous and futile effort besides—wasted effort." In fact, Luther eventually concluded the same about the pope, the Mass, pilgrimage, praying to saints, fraternities, purgatory, and the system of penance—all of which he believed were displacing Christ.

Introduction

While a monk, Luther also became a priest and so began saying mass. He was quickly identified by his brothers in the monastery as a leader, but Luther ended up on the wrong side of community politics and was sent away to the rather unpleasant town of Wittenberg with its new university—surrounded by mud and besotted with drinking. Luther pleaded with his superior and father-confessor Johann von Staupitz, "But it will be the death of me!" And so it was, in a way, but as Luther was about to undergo the hammer of God's left hand, so the university would never be the same—neither would the world for that matter. In short order, in 1512, he became a doctor by taking a public oath on the Bible to teach only true doctrine and identify those who taught falsehood. Within days he was set to teach Scripture, the highest of the disciplines, along with his many chores as preacher in several pulpits, reader at community meals, supervisor of monasteries, sayer of mass and of the daily hours of prayer, and writer of many letters.

In the middle of it all he began to hear a new voice in the very texts of Scripture that he was poring over. For all his religious and spiritual practices Luther was surprised to find what he called "the gospel," as something apart from "the law." Christ alone makes sinners right with God through faith *only*, that is, without any works of the law that we do. Once he began to catch this repeated publication of God's will in Scripture, theology could not go on as it had. Being a preacher, a sayer of mass, a judge of repentance, and an exhorter to good works all had to change in order to hand over the promises he was finding in the Bible.

Then he was quickly led to a series of amazing conclusions about the church practices he grew up with. The fact that in 1517 an "indulgence" preacher by the name of John Tetzel had set up shop nearby in Wittenberg was only

7

one of the reasons that Luther began to protest publicly. Indulgence, like purgatory or mass sacrifices, was an extension of two things: the authority of the pope to expand Scripture's teaching into areas of which it did not speak, and the growing practice of penance as a judgment of law rather than a promise of absolution as the end of sin. Luther began to reject both papacy and penance, at first slowly, then with steely and unfazed determination that continued throughout his life. Luther posted ninety-five theses on the church door in Wittenberg against the sale of indulgences that began with the famous words, "When our Lord and Master Jesus Christ said, 'Repent,' he willed the entire life of believers to be one of repentance."[2] He began to distinguish theologians who knew how to tell the difference between God's word as law and as gospel (theologians of the cross) from those like Tetzel who couldn't (theologians of glory).

By this time the pope and those at the Vatican began to

take notice of the obscure German monk. Luther was summoned to an interview with Cardinal Cajetan in the fall of 1518 and was asked to revoke his errors, including his statements on indulgences, the authority of the pope over Scripture, and being justified by faith alone. He did not revoke them, even though the cardinal threatened imprisonment, excommunication from the church, and worse.

Luther then entered a series of years with both intense concentration on Scripture and intense pressure from the outside to quit teaching as he was. On behalf of his new cause, Luther produced writings around 1520 that are often acknowledged as his greatest: *The Babylonian Captivity of the Church* concerned the church's sacramental system and how the sacraments could be opened anew by the gospel; the *Address to the Christian Nobility of the German Nation* denied that priests constituted a special class, but claimed that their authority to forgive made all believers into priests of Christ's kingdom; and *The Freedom of a Christian* described how a Christian was both sinner and saint at the same time, made righteous only on account of Christ, and how once a tree is made good, good fruit comes forth to serve the needs of others.

But the 1520s also saw great pressure from the outside placed on Luther. Luther was largely protected by his territory's prince, the Elector Frederick the Wise of Saxony. Frederick cared both for the truth of theological matters and that no German citizen or teacher at his university should be mistreated by the lofty powers. Despite the protection of the Elector, by 1521 Luther was an outlaw twice over—once in the eyes of the Vatican, and then after his famous trial at the German city of Worms, also in the eyes of the Holy Roman Empire and its king, Charles V. The papal announcement, or "bull," called "Arise, Lord, and judge your cause" (*Exsurge Domine*) was published in the summer of 1520 as the means by which to excommunicate Luther from the church. By the next spring Luther was ordered to appear before the emperor for his trial, which ended with Luther's refusal to recant his writings: "Here I stand. I can do no other. God help me! Amen!"

Luther was quite sure it would end with him as it had previous reformers, such as the Bohemian John Hus, and that he would be burned at the stake for heresy. But on his return trip to Wittenberg to await his end, the Elector Frederick arranged for Luther to be kidnapped from his wagon and hidden in one of the Elector's castles, the Wartburg. Luther did not like the idea at first, but used the time to translate the Bible into German, since he recognized that Scripture was not to be reserved for gnostics but publicized widely as God's own words to sinners.

The University of Wittenberg and the New Churches

On one side, Luther fought the old religion that buried Christ with its papacy, masses, penance, and monks. On the other, Luther began seeing the first of a series of "reformers," who became nothing more than tyrants trying to purify the church or who pushed for violent rebellion against political rulers. Luther's colleague at the university, Andreas Carlstadt, was one of the first to make reform nothing more than coercion, but right on his heels was Thomas Müntzer, who became a leader in the Peasants' War of 1524–1525. The most troubling aspect of such reforming tyrants (Luther called them "fanatics") was not even the terror they instilled but the mystical "revelations" they supposedly received from God. How can you argue with someone who believes he is God's new instrument of the Spirit because he has received visions and special messages from heaven, as Müntzer did? Müntzer told the peasants that bullets from the princes would be caught in his coat sleeve and that their uprising would succeed. Neither was true. His peasant uprising was put down mercilessly and Müntzer was executed. Coercion and tyranny could also come from reformers, Luther learned, and so he finally determined it was time to return to Wittenberg with the real authority of his reforms—he *preached* both the law and the gospel. God's changes would come through words. He told his congregations that love does not coerce, it serves. Faith comes by Christ's promise alone, and so he gave them both God's judgment concerning their works and their Savior, Jesus Christ, apart from their works.

In this way, Luther assumed the leadership of the evangelical cause. It was the preached word that mattered, not class warfare or governments "purified" by violent rebellion. "I did nothing," Luther declared, "the Word did everything. If I had wanted to stir up trouble, I could have brought immense bloodshed on Germany. In fact, I could have started such a game that even the emperor would not have been safe."[3] Luther is still often criticized for the vehemence with which he denied rebellion as the way to gain some measure of political freedom for the downtrodden, especially since he did not deny the use of the sword to rulers as Scripture clearly taught. He did develop a form of resistance to authority but not one that would place the power of revenge in the hands of "the people," whoever they may be.

From his return to Wittenberg in 1522 to his death in 1546, Luther exercised his vocation as teacher of the church and constantly fought the papal party on one side and the "fanatical" reformers on the other with his words. He preached, lectured on Scripture, debated opponents, and ministered to the needs of individuals and churches. In short, he helped transform churches into assemblies where the gospel was preached, and so were called "evangelical"—churches that eventually would spread around the world and continue to the present day.

CHAPTER ONE

In the Beginning . . . a Preacher:
What Is Proclamation?

And how are they to hear without someone to proclaim him?

(Romans 10:14)

Inside Out

Since the time of Socrates, thinkers have begun with what they do not know and from uncertainty have tried to gain some sure knowledge of "that which does not change." Skepticism is the main engine of knowledge, making sure that one does not build on a false foundation. Doubt alone may be able to discover truth (depending upon how skeptical one becomes), but it should at least destroy untruth. This method always begins deeply inside a person who sets aside the many outside influences and gets to work on what seems real—"the examined life," Socrates called it. Descartes called it his "meditations," when, exhausted by religious wars with no end in sight, he one day put his feet up on the warm woodstove and began to wield his instrument of doubt.

Theology typically works this way too. It goes inside people and tries to find some power in them that it calls an "image of God" or "vestige of the Trinity" that is somehow not overthrown by sin—something that we just couldn't possibly doubt—and then it builds its system of thought by adding God's "revelation" from Scripture to complete what it found. Theologians have joined philosophers in identifying the one true thing inside people as "free will." But for Luther this was not just a bad place to begin thinking; it was the source of every single sin, the fashioner of every single sinner, and the direct opponent of God. He called it "enthusiasm," God within-ism, which refuses to start with the word from a preacher sent by God and so cooks up some peculiar religion of the self. Adam and Eve did it, and so it is the *original* sin. It is also the sin that is repeated in ever evolving mutations of the same basic problem. It is theology curved in upon itself that only succeeds in declaring to the world what one finds while gazing at one's own navel.

Luther began *outside* a person, where certainty can only be *received*. He began with the Holy Spirit, whom he said "delights in assertions," meaning a "constant adhering, affirming, confessing, maintaining, and an invincible persevering."[1] Adhering is to stick like glue to something outside. Persevering is hanging on for dear life. Already this is strange language for truth, but it gets stranger. The Holy Spirit "calls, gathers, enlightens and sanctifies"[2] sinners who cannot save themselves or relate properly to God, Luther wrote in his famous *Small Catechism*. For that matter, sinners cannot really know anything but the sinking feeling that the world is completely messed up and we are caught in the mess. So the Holy Spirit enlightens us not by working with what is already inside of us, as if we had the truth hidden in seed and it only needed to be nurtured by a talented guru or delivered by Plato's midwife.

Outside In

In truth, Luther thought, the Holy Spirit sends a *preacher*. Preachers are sent with God's word as if from a far country bearing the message over the mountains by their "beautiful feet," as the preacher Isaiah once put it. They do not bring advice, or a spiritual method of getting in touch with God, or the idea that "the truth is already in you" and you just need to get in touch with your inner light. The preacher announces "news." News is "new" to you. News is not an idea or problem or riddle; it is an announcement of what God has already done. In other words, it announces a decision. Surprisingly, the news of this decision comes in the form of two historic events. The first is that God has judged the world and you in it and found it trapped under evil with no way out. The "day of the Lord," as the Bible describes the final judgment, has already arrived when the preacher comes. That is "bad" news. But God's preacher says more. Apart from this judgment, God did a new thing by raising Jesus Christ from the dead. He forgives you, because of his Son Jesus Christ's victory over death. The Holy Spirit sends a preacher to give you Jesus Christ as forgiveness of sin and the promise of new creation. That is good, albeit unexpected, news.

If this particular sort of preacher does not come, you are lost inside yourself, racked by doubts and skepticism, since all is apparently "relative" to the peculiar insides of whoever is speaking. It is true we can control the confusion this skepticism causes by practicing toleration for others and their differences. But if toleration is all we have, then in the end it is just like the wise man said: "Vanity of vanities, all is vanity" (Eccl. 1:2). The apostle Paul used stronger language yet. For without a preacher God gives up humans to what is within them: lusts, degrading their bodies, exchanging truths of God for lies, and becoming so confused about worship (giving God his due) that everything

gets turned upside down—so we worship creatures and manipulate God for our own ends (Rom. 1:24–25).

For Luther, truth is more like hanging on for dear life to the preached word than it is searching within and weighing different possibilities while we suspend final judgment. Truth is trust and a right relationship with the real God, who is decidedly outside ourselves but has come near in preaching. If we have anything to say to each other beyond our own likes or dislikes (our "tastes" or "perspectives"), then what we say must come from God's word that interrupts us—breaking us out of our caves with an *external* promise that comes *into* the heart. For example, take this powerful promise from Scripture: "Everyone who calls on the name of the LORD shall be saved" (Joel 2:32). Now reason backward from this, as the apostle Paul did: "But how are they to call on one in whom they have not believed? And how are they to believe in one of whom they have never heard? And how are they to hear without someone to proclaim him? And how are they to proclaim him unless they are sent? As it is written, 'How beautiful are the feet of those who bring good news!'" Then Paul concluded with what became Luther's theology in a nutshell: "So faith comes from what is heard, and what is heard comes through the word of Christ" (Rom. 10:14–17).

Beginning something, Luther liked to say (whether beginning a theology or one's own life), is always beginning again. So we begin with God's word as law and gospel but never advance beyond it. Yet the Spirit's work is not only to see that a preacher is sent but that hearers trust the announcement as *belonging* to them. In this way, Scripture is abundantly clear about what God promises, to whom such promises apply, and by whom they are rightly given. By this means, Luther undoes mere methods of *interpretation* of Scripture and existential theories of meaning because the Holy Spirit sends a preacher to you with words that fit—words that you could never have come up with no matter how long you stared at your navel.

God's Permanent Interruption

Two of the most famous phrases from the Bible begin with "In the beginning." The first is Genesis 1:1 (the first line of the Bible): "In the beginning God *created.* . . ." The second is the first line of the story of Jesus Christ in the Gospel of John: "In the beginning was the *Word.*" Martin Luther understood that God not only started and preserved the world's course by speaking but *interrupted* it by speaking a new word. God makes no apology for the abrupt interruption and speaks out of anger and determination in light of what humans have done to creation. The interruption is decisive with the crucifixion of Jesus Christ, the Son of the Father. Precisely what God says by way of the interruption tears open the world, revealing it as old (and coming to an end) in the light of his new creation already begun with Christ: "This is my beloved Son; listen to him." The world's powers, divided every which way among themselves by culture and personal taste, nevertheless *unite* to oppose Jesus Christ's message: "The time is fulfilled, and the kingdom of God has come near; repent, and believe in the good news" (Mark 1:15).

Only the weak and cast-off, the terrorized, unclean, powerless, prostitutes, tax collectors, and sinners generally have any ear for Jesus—since they have almost nothing left to lose and a terrific amount to gain if he really can forgive sin and conquer death. So, for the present, God's interrupting words are held in faith by God's sinners. Faith means the words are hidden to sight, but will be seen on the final day of Christ's victory over "this evil world" (Gal.

1:4). That victory is for the sake of the Holy Spirit's new creation when the mighty are brought down from their thrones and the lowly are lifted up (Mary sang that in Luke 1 and Miriam in 1 Samuel 2). That means that God's words are always distinguished as two kinds: *judgment* of what is old, not right, and without any future, and *promise* that establishes Christ's new world of forgiven sinners as right, new, and eternally alive. Theology and life itself must be understood entirely according to this distinction of old and new. When it comes to us sinners, that means, "the Lord kills and brings to life" (1 Sam. 2:6).

Admittedly this description sounds odd to most anyone on first hearing—or second for that matter. It is a peculiar type of what theologians call "eschatological" (having to do with last things) or even "apocalyptic" (having to do with God's final judgment). Yet the real problem this poses is not those unusual words. Luther understood that God's decisive interruption of this life opposes basic beliefs that are tiresomely outmoded:

- That the world is progressing toward a higher goal;

- That people are what they do;

- That humans are continually existing, independent subjects actively transcending themselves (reaching higher, climbing the ladder, pursuing their dreams, or every day in every way getting better and better);

- That freedom means either creating our own destinies or is just dumb luck (fate and chance);

- That God rewards chosen people with prosperity and punishes the undeserving losers (merit system);

- That death can be overcome with good behavior (following the golden rule) or mystical participation in God's being (falling like a tiny drop into the great ocean of life)—if not at first then on repeated tries (such as in reincarnation).

More often than not, following these little rules of life is what we mean by living a "good," "moral," or "spiritual" life. In glaring contrast to this, Luther saw that the world deludes itself with dreams of progress while it violently opposes God's own words, and that humans are not continually existing subjects who become right and holy by gradually doing greater works of the law. Instead, God's word reveals the world's evil and darkness, not because creation's material "stuff" is evil, or even its laws or offices or powers are evil (old Manicheism), but because the world's *faith* is put in the wrong place. Luther understood that all those who come after the death and resurrection of God's only Son are in "the latter days," in which faith alone holds Christ as "right" and "certain," while awaiting the last day. On that day all will be seen that is now held in faith. But for now, everything in theology must be marked by the struggle between old and new in this world.

Luther then asserted that faith is constantly under attack by the powers of this old world: the devil, the world, and our sinful selves. He observed, to the horror of many, that God *himself* (outside of his words, outside Christ) attacks us, "cooking and roasting his saints," as he once said, so that faith in Christ's promise of forgiveness given for you by a preacher remains your only deliverance from death to life. That is what it feels like to be in these "latter days," in which we either wait perilously for the other shoe of judgment to drop (by fate or chance), or with eager anticipation await seeing what now is held only in faith—that God

is right in declaring his opponents forgiven on account of Christ. We can get a start on the theological fun ahead when we begin to pose Luther's contrast to the world's dreams this way:

- The world is not progressing; it is ending and being created new.
- People are not what they do, but what God calls them.
- Humans are not continually existing subjects of self-transcendence but are passive before God. They are killed and raised, and so they never advance beyond baptism.
- Freedom is not creating our destiny (even with God's help) with free will, but is trust given by the Holy Spirit in Christ that makes us lords of everything and servants to all.
- Jesus was a loser among "winners" and put to death for it; yet the cross became a new kind of victory over self-righteous sinners.
- Death is not overcome by works but by Christ—crucified, raised, and given to his own betrayers as forgiveness of sin, decisively in the Lord's Supper.

Perhaps no people need this challenge to their assumptions more than Americans, with their manifest destiny, winner-takes-all sense of being chosen by God because they deserve it.

CHAPTER TWO

Law and Gospel:
God's Two Words

"Look! Here is the Lamb of God!"

(John 1:36)

The Mouth and Finger of John: Two Absolutes

On the fourth Sunday in Advent, 1533, Luther preached
to his family and friends on the Gospel text from the evangelist John about another John, the forerunner and

preacher of Christ. This passage is a brief, pointed example of what a preacher sent by the Holy Spirit actually preaches. After all, many people put themselves forward as learned teachers, inspired saints, or bearers of secrets they have received. How do you tell true preachers from those selling their own snake oil? The Old Testament had a way of "testing the spirits": If what the preacher promised came true, it was God's word. Luther applied that to the New Testament and observed that true preaching gives all to Jesus Christ so that "this man should be all in all." A simple test can be put to preachers (simple in words, hard in practice): Does the preacher make as much of Christ as his heavenly Father and the Holy Spirit do? The Father sends his Son, holding nothing back. The Holy Spirit witnesses to Jesus Christ alone without any remainder. They give everything to Christ. Everything? Yes, everything. So Luther began his sermon like this:

> For God resolved that this man should be all in all; whoever comes to him will find redemption from sin, death, and hell. This man is all things; he is the way, the truth, and the life; through him alone all patriarchs, prophets, and apostles from the beginning of the world have been saved. This John the Baptist well knows. For this reason he steers people away from himself to this man, so that they will not ignore so great a treasure.[1]

Already you can see the difficulty. If there is anything that bothers post-Enlightenment thinkers it is the notion of an absolute. But here we find not just one absolute but two. What is the sum total of everything the world has to offer *to God* (Luther called it *coram deo*, "before the face of God")? What measures up to God's standard or law? What is holy? Nothing. Nothing at all. In fact, what it has pro-

duced is not only imperfect, but before God is sin—not because it was created badly but because it has led to trusting other gods instead of Jesus Christ.

I suppose the most dramatic rendering of this has always been the first three chapters of the apostle Paul's letter to the Romans. There Paul asserts that God will "repay according to each one's deeds," and since Christ's death, that repayment is no longer in doubt: "All have sinned and fall short of the glory of God" (Rom. 3:23). All? *All*. No one knows this or believes this before it is preached by a true preacher, and it always comes as something harsh and deadly: "We are to do good works and work hard at doing them," Luther preached, "for God has so enjoined and commanded in the Ten Commandments. But when it comes to this man who is

25

called Christ, you should humble yourself like John, and throw all the good works you have ever done at his feet and frankly admit that you are not fit to wipe off Christ's shoes."[2] Yet, strangely, even all of this that we and the world have produced are counted as *sins* and are given over to Jesus Christ, and he (more strangely yet) takes them as his own where they nailed him to the cross and die on him. That is not mystical to Luther. Just as his friends and followers abandoned Christ on the night he was betrayed, and just as some actually drove nails into his hands, presently people actually reject Christ by really and truly rejecting his preacher when that preacher comes for them. Preaching this first absolute is called preaching the *law*. It brings hearers to their end before God, and their true death under God's eternal judgment. Death is, after all, being unable to do anything more. Once this preaching ends, there is nothing left to do. Remember, this is brought or preached to you from outside. It is not a feeling you have of being worthless. It is *news*, and it magnifies sin beyond what you feel or think could really be the case, but does so according to God's judgment on the matter instead of your own.

But I said there were *two* absolutes; the first is that you have *no* righteousness before God in yourself and *all* that you have and are is counted as sin. The second is greater yet, as Luther says: "Let us look to the mouth and finger of John with which he bears witness and points, so that we do not close our eyes to or lose our Lord and Savior, Jesus Christ."[3] John used his big, long, bony index finger to point away from himself and to Christ: "Behold the lamb of God who takes away the sin of the world." Christ forgives all your sin by giving you *his own righteousness*, which raises you from the dead. Luther used three essential words to describe a sinner's "translation" from the kingdom of sin and death to the kingdom of righteousness and life—

Christ, faith, and *imputation. Christ* alone is righteous before the heavenly Father. *Christ* takes your sin with its killing judgment and covers it so the Father forgets it. When the heavenly Father then comes to judge you at the last day he beholds only his Son, and what his Son *imputes,* or applies to you, is his *own* righteousness. You do not see this in the form of holiness in your own self. *Faith* alone clings to Christ.

There are several ways that Luther put this central teaching of the Bible. First, there is not one but two kinds of righteousness. That itself should disturb you, as if God were using two different scorecards, one for the regular law that everybody has naturally in the sense of wrong and right and the other for the righteousness that is a sheer gift that comes from hearing God's promises. "Jesus Christ is not a new Moses" was another way Luther described the

basic preaching of the New Testament. Christ doesn't bring a better law; he brings something really new. But when it came to describing this as doctrine Luther usually called it preaching "justification by faith alone, apart from works of the law." For him, that is not just one more teaching used by the church but the very thing on which Christ's new kingdom of forgiven sinners, the church, stands or falls—"the chief article." He meant in part that this is the test of a true preacher: Either justification by faith alone in Christ is what gets preached or the preacher is false.

In the middle of this sermon Luther asked the question that must be asked about his whole theological legacy: "I, Dr. Martin, am already—God be praised!—excommunicated and condemned to death. Why are they so antagonistic toward us? Why can't they tolerate us?"[4] Neither the church nor the world tolerated him, though both are extremely good at tolerating most everything else that has the slightest hint of "righteousness" about its cause. Luther thought the reason was clear. Neither the world nor the church wants all of its stuff to be nothing (or worse) before God. Unlike John, they will not confess, "I am not worthy to untie his sandal," nor will they say that Christ alone is the one on whom God has put all sin in order to conquer it.

So what happens to one who actually comes preaching like John or Luther? The world, and the church that has become like the world, tries to kill the messenger, just like it did to Jesus Christ, because the message is doubly offensive: First, it is *indiscriminately inclusive* (all have sinned); second, it is *narrowly exclusive* (only Christ) and all out of your hands as something the Father, Son, and Holy Spirit do for you. Worse yet, it is not only out of your hands; it is literally over your dead body. You cannot get more provocative than that. That is, unless you start asking questions like: What if someone doesn't get such a preacher? What if the Holy Spirit starts selecting some and not others? What then of your God? God doesn't play dice, right? God can't be that unfair, or put so much weight on something so small as a preached word or a first-century Hebrew peasant, right? What about free will? If you take justification by faith alone that distinguishes law and gospel as your center point, then isn't everything in the world turned upside down?

Before we take up the legitimate questions that must follow such a preacher, I want to put a little more meat on the bones of what Luther calls the "chief article" or central teaching of all Christianity—*justification by faith alone apart from works of the law*. This requires a basic distinction between what Luther calls "law" and "gospel."

Ontology: Singing Monotone

When a tone-deaf person sings, it can be painful to hear. But if you have to listen to theologians who know only the one note of the law, it is not only painful but deadly. They like to describe the big picture of God's plan for humans as a test to see whether you will pass. They explain God's mind or the order of God's plan for salvation and how you can fit in *if* you follow the rules of the game that God plays. Then the church and its leaders act as referees deciding who is in and who is out of salvation by passing or failing some test. Thinking this way makes it impossible to grasp what Luther is saying when he distinguishes law and gospel as what is old and done for and what is newly arriving with Jesus Christ.

Sometimes thinking only according to the one word of law means thinking *ontologically*, by which all beings in nature are imagined to exist in some grand hierarchy, or chain of being, that extends from God all the way down to the lowliest stone. Sometimes it means imagining a grand legal and mystical notion of history such as the popular myth that everything in life goes out from God and then returns in a sweep of events that God uses to learn who he really is—an exit and return that is repeated in miniature here among individuals. Sometimes thinking only according to the law means thinking *teleologically,* in which life begins in a seed and expands to its goal to become, for example, a fully developed oak tree or person. The simplest form of law alone in theology I suppose is that created nature itself is grace, or God's favor, and the human problem is that we haven't recognized it or responded to it. If that were the case, then humans would be rid of their problems if they could just convince themselves that they are beautiful, good, and worthy in and of themselves. But as you may have learned, affirming yourself is a lonely and endless enterprise.

Unless these ontological worlds are turned upside down or split in two and a new way of thinking enters that breaks out of the monotone about law, Luther always remains a curious puzzle or heretic. Worse yet, you end up thinking God put you on earth to test you and is even now waiting to see if you pass. Then the questions from inside really pile up. Which religion is the best? Maybe none at all? How do I know I have followed God's plan? How can I be sure I will reach the goal? Are there any do-overs or extra credit for this test? Perhaps there is no God, or I myself am God?

Any and all of these legal Johnny-one-notes hide an ontological description of life that ends up being what some have called a "ladder theology." That means we are put *down* here on earth to climb some spiritual ladder *up* as our way of getting back to God. Without any exception that I know, these various theories consider the basic stuff, being, or substance of a human being to be the unicorn of all theology: a free will. This imaginary "substance" or "communion" with God through the will is supposed to be the thing that gets you up the ladder (or what is its mirror image—the attempt to empty oneself so completely that God considers the abnegation worthy of a reward). It doesn't really matter if this way of thinking is more Protestant and individualistic or more Roman Catholic and collective. You may talk more about your personal relationship with Jesus or about becoming initiated into the church, but the basic structure of the relation between you and God remains the same. Philipp Melanchthon, Luther's fellow teacher and friend at Wittenberg, once called this situation "singling out the law," because it was unable to grasp that Scripture has two words, not one: law and gospel.[5]

For Luther, singling out the law is like someone with a tin ear trying to sing the great song of Christ. Everything that comes out endlessly repeats the one note of your own obedience to God's command: "You have to decide for Christ" or "You have to be obedient to the rule of faith in communion with the church." And always such a monotone ceases singing about Christ and takes up what Walt Whitman once celebrated as "The Song of Myself." Johnny-one-notes always sing to God about their own selves and what they are going to do, and yet *nothing gets done*. It is like the husband who keeps promising his wife that the garage will get cleaned. God cannot stand the stink this self-righteousness sends up to heaven, Luther thought, because it always leaves Christ standing out of the action like an old, unused van parked beside the driveway.

Two Notes, Not One

One of the first consequences of a theology that actually thinks beyond the law is that preoccupation with the

human will disappears. The opponent of God, according to Luther, is not a free will sowing its wild oats but is the devil and death itself. For years now, talking about the devil and a catastrophic end to the world has seemed irrational. Hellfire and brimstone preaching, such as Jonathan Edwards's sinner dangling by a thread, was attributed to the work of charlatans like Elmer Gantry or to TV evangelists. I admit there is something strange about the notions of the devil and the end of time. A reasonable person naturally prefers attributing evil to chance events, the evil designs of a human will, or the final test of one's faith. But in a fateful attempt to move from one legalism to another, reason assigned Satan to cultural "myth," or the projection of frightened minds attempting to explain things their science had failed to grasp. They were also singing monotone.

Then one of the most advanced cultures of the world perpetrated a holocaust of Jews and other "types" of people, and at the same time a nuclear age began. People had to begin pondering the wholesale destruction of people, the earth, and perhaps more. The devil, who never minds lack of publicity, started to enter again into language that could not reduce evil to misuse of free will. Luther could not imagine taking God seriously without also taking the devil seriously, and he could not imagine what sense you could make of God's word without being aware of how God is ending the old world and beginning the new. Time was not just a long line leading to perfection or stretching infinitely without known beginning or end. Those are what Luther would understand to be "myths" used to cover up the real truth about one's own impending death and judgment by God. Instead, everything for Luther was marked by the distinction of "old" and "new," because Christ justifies sinners apart from the law. Understanding this cannot be done merely as a historian; the great philosopher Hegel

once called such theologians "bean counters," who kept accounts of other people's wealth but had no assets of their own. But neither can it be done scientifically or rationally by investigating the human possibility of knowing God, or feeling God, or willfully choosing God. Like it or not, Luther has plentiful "assets." For him, investigating God means you are already in trouble—and so the only way to learn to swim is to jump right into the deep end.

Cosmic Rebellion

Luther's most famous words have come down to us in the form of a hymn, "A Mighty Fortress Is Our God":

> A mighty fortress is our God,
> A sword and shield victorious;
> He breaks the cruel oppressor's rod
> And wins salvation glorious.[6]

That hymn is both a paraphrase of Psalm 46 and a sermon on the text. Luther took the words from the psalm as

God's apocalyptic curse and promise (two absolutes). Luther believed he stood under God in the middle of a great cosmic battle in which this old, evil world was being led by its cruel oppressor ("the old evil foe") in a final, cataclysmic upheaval. It was the dying convulsion of a great rebellion against the Creator that would make the mountains shake in the heart of the sea, the waters roar, and the earth itself come to an end. In this old world, Luther found himself and all others under the sway of that old evil foe next to whom no man or woman could ever be a match ("on earth he has no equal").

God's great weapon to fight the devil and sinners (along with their idols) is his *word* that comes to us at the right time—incarnate, deep in the flesh of Jesus Christ. Christ's great weapon is the tiniest, weakest, and apparently most ethereal thing in this old world—a word. "Sticks and stones may break my bones, but words can never hurt me"

is usually our mothers' first lesson in ancient ontology. Jesus proves it to be a lie when it comes to God. Jesus came forgiving. This word is first an absolute judgment on all that fights against Christ, and second it is an absolute promise that Christ not only wins but does so for *your own sake*; he is on your side. It is conveyed right to your doorstep in the simple pronouncement of the forgiveness of your sin. For Luther, all of Scripture and all of the mystery of God's will, destiny, or fate itself (as frightened creatures often put it) is the forgiveness of sin. This little word subdues the mighty devil, who cannot help but let it stand where God puts it into the world, though he storms and rages.

So, for Luther, what has God done to save sinners who rebelled and fell under the power of Satan? Everything. God has done all. "Justification by faith alone" is shorthand for the faith that finally declares God to be right in this unbelievable act of forgiveness for you. Faith alone gives God his due, and so Luther sang God's song with more than one note of law.

CHAPTER THREE

Justification by Faith Alone

For in it [i.e. the gospel] the righteousness of God is revealed through faith for faith; as it is written, "The one who is righteous will live by faith."

(Romans 1:17)

If everyone needs a preacher to hear and hearing makes faith in Christ, how did Luther come to hear God as he did? Where did Luther's theology come from? Of course he grew up in the church, but as Luther observed, what he was taught was *burying* rather than *giving* Christ—even

Luther for Armchair Theologians

when it spoke incessantly about him. Two things are clear from the massive research into Luther's theological break-through. First, Luther had predecessors who helped form his theology, especially the biblical commentators running from Jerome to Biel. But, secondly, Luther was not just one more reformer. He did not give birth to a new school of thought within the Roman church as Occam, Aquinas, or the Conciliarists had. Nor was he a Wycliff or Hus, two early reformers in the best sense of that word who sought to change church practices. Such prior reformers never found the distinction of law and gospel as Luther did.

Luther's Cause

Throughout his life Luther frequently had occasion to reflect upon the beginning of this cause. One day at his table Luther put it succinctly: "When I found this distinction between law and gospel, I *broke through*."[1] Consequently, Luther was certain that God wanted more from him than church reform. God transferred him violently from a false lord to a true one, and so was changing his *hope* by killing and raising him. Then Luther thought that God did not whisk him off to heaven but planted him deeply in the world as a divine mask through which God administered the single effective medicine for sick souls: *faith toward God and love toward neighbor.*

Theology preceding Luther had become a long tradition of intertwining and confusing law and gospel whether it was the theology taught at the time in the schools, called *scholasticism,* or that coming from the monastic orders, including mysticism. Luther went with this distinction of law and gospel right into the church's creeds and the Bible itself and judged all teaching by what each and every sentence had to say about Jesus Christ. When a text gave

Christ as the justifier of sinners, it was God's own gospel word; Paul and John, Isaiah and Moses stood out in this regard. When it made Christ a judge or ignored him altogether, as in James, Luther called it "straw." To this day, Luther's display of biblical criticism and criticism of church history is astounding. Who would dare say today that a book in the Bible is good for cleaning up animal pens?

A Rare Bird

Luther was once goaded late in his life into writing a tiny autobiography called *The Preface to the Latin Writings* to go along with a collection of his "greatest theological hits" being prepared for publication. Luther used the occasion as a kind of look back at how "our cause," as he called it, began. "At first," he reminded his readers, "I was all alone. . . . I got into these turmoils by accident and not by will or intention."[2] At first, being alone was Luther's constant temptation that the church leaders paraded before him: "Are you the only one who knows?" Luther had to go through the fires with that question ringing in his ears, and it finally made him locate the one sure thing on which to stand: Christ alone makes sinners right only by faith—apart from the law—or all is lost. It didn't matter how many people in the church opposed it or if a council or even a book in the Bible said something different. Luther often remembered the famous moment in the fourth century when the whole church leadership had been reduced exactly to three nonheretical bishops who did not give in to the false teacher Arius, and he concluded that at times the true church has been made up only of baptized infants who have not yet been corrupted by bad teaching! Numbers and age do not determine the truth for preaching.

More recently, Luther's uniqueness has been taken as a matter of his peculiar personality. Much has been written about Luther's psychological state or the social conditions of the peasants in the late Middle Ages that does not explain Luther. We can actually be refreshed by hearing Luther's own description of his circumstance. He says he was *taken captive*—not by an inner longing or deep feelings of guilt or by revolutionary zeal but by "an extraordinary ardor for understanding Paul in the Epistle to the Romans."[3] This was no inner struggle but decidedly an outer one, and stranger yet, Luther's cause started with one little word: *righteousness.*

He found that word in the apostle Paul's statement to the Romans that "the one who is righteous will live by faith" (Rom. 1:17 quoting Habakkuk). Luther was a rare bird because he took this biblical word so seriously that it killed him, much like he later wrote to a sick friend, "You are one of those rare birds who take the Word of God very seriously and are faithful to the Kingdom of

Christ."[4] We have a hard time grasping this, since for us texts are things that merely express a person's opinion, and we can take them or leave them. But for Luther, Paul just stood there implacably with an external address to a congregation fifteen hundred years in the past, saying something that was utterly upsetting for the world order that Luther was taught. Paul wouldn't let Luther have what Luther wanted—a simple formula of grace + faith + love + works = salvation. Instead, Paul said faith = salvation. So Luther tried violently to get rid of Paul as if the apostle was an obstacle to freedom, but Paul could not be moved.

It is important to note that Luther's was no introspective consciousness that made him feel guilty about himself, nor was he merely dealing with personal demons. He would sound like a braggart to us now rather than a troubled and tender man in need of affirmation: "I lived as a monk without reproach," he said. Luther was not a man looking at his navel or judging himself in any way; he was judging Scripture by accusing Paul of preaching dangerous nonsense. "Thus," he says, "I raged with a fierce and troubled conscience." Luther was in the throes of learning that a conscience is not the moral compass of an active will that points us in the direction of the right thing to do. Conscience is the passive form of *being located* in the world. A conscience is the means by which God gives people place in the world through calling them by name. It is an experience of "being captured" or of being captivated by one's supposed enemy, and so conscience is never a solitary or individual matter but is God's relation to you as his creature *through words*. Luther's own conscience became a battleground for what he would shortly call "the gospel." Being captured by God was going to mean both death and life, both law and gospel.

Beating on Paul

In his day the church was saying plenty of things about the word "righteousness," but Luther began to realize that it reversed Paul's meaning. The church institution and its tradition in history were not adequate to the gospel even though the job of the church was to hand over God's message of how to become righteous. The church's inadequacy felt to Luther like an earthquake while he was in the process of falling into the hands of the living God (Heb. 10:31). Scripture was taking on a whole new face for him, but this was not merely a change of perspectives. Luther believed he was undergoing a translation from death to life, being dragged from one lord to another in unexpected violence.

What did Paul want by preaching the righteousness of God as he did? Even today we have a hard time hearing this since we are not a blank slate when it comes to our personal identities. We come from the womb with a notion of how to judge ourselves as "right." We usually think of righteousness in terms of discrete acts, such as answering a teacher's question correctly: "You're right," she might say. Or we try *righting* a wrong done to a victim of a crime. But when it comes time to take account of a whole life and we ask what makes a life worth living (as Socrates put it) or what gives one's soul peace, then we turn to a long history of common reflections by philosophers and theologians: "Neither evening nor morning star is so wonderful as justice," said Aristotle.[5] Immanuel Kant practically sang it out: "Duty! Thou sublime and mighty name . . . only holdest forth a law which of itself finds entrance into the mind . . . from which to be descended is the indispensable condition of the only worth which men can give themselves."[6]

"Just" and "right" are words whose meaning comes

from the experience of making a building, as when a stonemason drops down a plumb line to see if a wall is straight and says, "She's true" or "She's right." That language was picked up for how a judge determines guilt or innocence in a court trial, and so when the judge declares a verdict we say that on this day "justice was done." What Luther discovered was that these words also had another root in experience—the final experience of the cemetery where the dead are laid in graves and the living all wonder how they will fare at the *final judgment*. Perhaps more commonly today we simply shrug and ask, "Is that all there is?" Often survivors of a deceased friend have strong feelings that death is just not right or not fair, but what can you do about it?

When Luther went to Scripture he had just this kind of baggage in tow regarding righteousness. He assumed, as

the philosophers had taught, that to *be* right was to *do* right. And to do right was measured by God's own eternal law that has set up the order of true and worthy living. So when Luther came upon Paul's phrase "righteousness of God," he believed he knew what it meant: There is a right and wrong way to live according to God's plan, like a blueprint for a building or a code of law for a judge. God was being right whenever God exercised *judgment* according to divine *law*. God applied merit or reward where someone had done well, and wrath or punishment when someone had done evil.

So you could take "righteousness of God" in Paul's little sentence to mean an attribute of God that describes his being according to his own law. That is, justice could be taken as a subjective genitive that names a thing belonging to God. The Bible says, of course, that God is righteous and that this often contrasts with what humans think is right—"My thoughts are not your thoughts, nor are your ways my ways, says the LORD" (Isa. 55:8). Whoever God may be, whatever that God wants must be right. But what if God does something that seems utterly wrong? What if God killed people in an earthquake, or what if this God was the kind that chose Jacob (the cheater) over Esau the elder? In his letter to the Romans, Paul took up that famous case of injustice in the Old Testament story of God scandalously choosing Jacob and concluded, "Is there injustice on God's part? By no means!" But this amounts to simply repeating the obvious: God is right. God is God. Whatever God does must be right. That is what rhetoricians call a "tautology"; a subject and predicate being the same in a sentence doesn't really give you anything but a sheer abstraction. God is God; you are not. God is right. If he chose Jacob, God must have had a good, legal reason for doing so.

The key to Luther's distress, however, came in the next step. If God is always right, then what does he actually think of *me*? Where do *I* fit in? Philosophers and the religious have spoken with one voice on this matter. You and I "fit in" to God's big plan by the way we *participate* in God's justice, the way we *harmonize* with God's theme, or the way we *imitate* the will of God who then judges according to the law or order or structure that has been placed in the world as a kind of plumb line.

Aristotle Toppled

It was Aristotle who gave the formula that would plague Luther at this point, as he beat on Paul to understand what God thought of him. For Aristotle, to be just is to enjoy one's own possessions; to be unjust is to enjoy the possessions of others.[7] This is called "distributive justice," whereby equality or balance is maintained according to a kind of arithmetic. Who rightfully owns what? Of course, a judge is then the epitome of justice, taking from those who have ill-gotten gains and restoring to those whose goods have been taken. Isn't God like that, Luther thought? Isn't God the Supreme Court justice who will decide your guilt or innocence based on how well you have loved others?

Scripture abounds with descriptions of God as the just judge, righting the wrongs of this world—if not in this life then in the next. It is easy then to understand the little phrase "righteousness of God" as God giving to each his or her due. Christ himself would then act as the great judge, and indeed the common picture of Luther's day had Jesus sitting on a rainbow with a sword coming from his mouth (from a vision in the book of Revelation), ready to separate the sheep from the goats according to deeds done on earth. That was the way Luther was reading all of Scripture:

Christ is judge; he judges according to his law like that given through Moses, and God will then reward virtue and punish vice. The only question that ever remained was how *you* in particular will fare before God's final trial. Then God's gavel will descend. Bang! Justice is done. Did you do enough or not?

Then came his reading of Paul, where he says he finally considered "the context." If you took "the righteousness of God" out of context you could read it according to Aristotle rather nicely. It could even have certain religious advantages like motivation for behaving better. After all, it has been notoriously difficult for philosophers to convince themselves and others that being just is something good to

be. Why be just? Because even if you have momentary suc-
cess for being unjust in this world, in the end you will pay.
Thus, justice came to be equated with God's wrath or
anger at wrongdoing. God's wrath = God's justice. It was
a neat and practical formula for getting people to behave.
But it wasn't what Paul was preaching as "the gospel."

Luther noticed strange expressions that occurred only
in Paul's letters and nowhere else in Scripture in quite the
same way. Paul said that God's righteousness is "through
faith." Was that just another name for good deeds? No,
that doesn't work. Paul required you to make a distinction: "not having a righteousness of my own that comes
from the law, but one that comes through faith in Christ"
(Phil. 3:9). Two kinds of righteousness—how can that be?
It is like having two different rules or two sets of requirements. That can't be fair, can it? Then the final blow: "But
now, apart from law, the righteousness of God has been
disclosed" (Rom. 3:21). What could Paul possibly mean
by that? He not only began giving an entirely new description of righteousness by declaring something like two
kinds of being right; he seemed to say that the righteousness of God's law was in direct and vital opposition to
God's righteousness in Christ. Paul's context was describing two kinds of righteousness in a fight to the death! And
the loser is already clear—God's own righteous law and
God's wrathful judgment cannot make a person right.
Christ stands alone as a *new* righteousness, where he is,
the law is over and done with. More strangely yet, Christ's
righteousness is not only *his own,* but it is *given as a gift*
to the undeserving.

When a conscience that has located itself in this world by
the basic standard of law and distributive justice first comes
upon this, it sounds like gibberish. Then when Paul's con-
viction settles in, it sounds like hostility to the very order

of creation. Finally, if those words capture and hold the conscience long enough, it frightens a person with the feeling that the bottom just fell out of the universe. This is especially true for those who have been good at the law. That is why it hit Luther so hard. He was really good at the law. He was better than most everyone around and he knew it, since the standard is quite objective.

Faith Alone Saves

Luther then began to put two and two together. Paul was talking about a *new* kind of righteousness. God was doing a new thing, just as promised in the preacher Isaiah. He was doing this new thing in his Son Jesus Christ, specifically through Jesus' death on the cross. God's new righteousness was making the *unrighteous* right. God was doing what God "naturally" does, that is, creating out of nothing. He was acting with a freedom the world didn't anticipate that God had—to do something "right" outside of, and even against, his own law. "Righteousness of God," when taken in Paul's context of preaching, was what Luther began to hear as a genitive of the author. It was not what God *is* in himself as a substance but what God *gives* to sinners—it described a relationship to God. In Luther's own recounting of this, one can sense his excitement: "I ran through all of Scripture"—and what Paul was saying Luther finally saw throughout the Bible. Righteousness was what God gives, freely and without condition, to God's own *opponents.* You might consider God a fool for doing this—as Paul says, it is foolish according to the Gentiles. Or you may consider God as reneging on an agreement—Paul says Christ is a stumbling block for his own people, the Jews. Nevertheless, God has made himself right by giving away Christ's righteousness to people who *did not earn it*. God is just the kind of God who chooses the wrong ones, and that is what we have to swallow here on earth (swallow, that is, unless you are one of the wrong ones, in which case you grab what you can without fussing).

And how is it that this faith that is made by God as righteousness apart from the law comes? It comes by a simple promise. Reason is bewildered at this. It comes *apart* from deeds, apart from judging and giving to each according to what is due; it comes apart from merit, wrath, punishment,

and the law; it is apart from harmonies, various participations in God's being, equalities of material and spiritual goods, virtues, morality, orders, systems, and reason itself. The Father makes right in this old world *only* by raising his crucified Son from the dead and giving that Son to his enemies as a gift that comes in the form of a simple promise "for you." Nothing could remain the same if that were true—not the identification of a self, or of God, or of what is "good" or "true" or "right" or, for that matter, what the course of history itself is. Even the source of human problems and misery would have to change as well as the most ardently sought and least understood of all human desires: *freedom.*

A deconstruction and a new construction were underway in Luther's "cause" that make the masters of suspicion such as Freud, Marx, and Nietzsche pale in comparison. A new commonplace or locus was emerging that was not there in prior philosophy or rhetoric because those were built on ontology's one note of the law. Of course, the word "faith" was not new in Luther's day, but Luther's use of it was. He once wrote to his friend and colleague, Philipp Melanchthon, at the moment when the Evangelical cause was being made before the emperor and world in the form of the Augsburg Confession in June 1530. Justification of the ungodly that distinguishes two kinds of righteousness and two preaching offices, law and gospel, was put forward as the clear and universal declaration of Christian faith by Luther's evangelical party. But it was rejected by the emperor and papal representatives, and the consequences looked dire for the evangelicals. Luther then wrote to encourage his friend Melanchthon in this way:

> You are torturing yourself about the end and outcome of the cause because you cannot comprehend them. If you could comprehend them, I should not

like to be a participant, much less the author, of this cause. God has put it in a certain commonplace which you do not have in your rhetoric or in your philosophy. This is faith. And in this faith are comprehended all the things that are not seen and do not appear. . . . May the Lord increase your faith and the faith of all of us.[8]

Faith in Christ's promise, not works of the law, alone saves. But we will have to be very careful, since the word "faith" is one of the most abused words in our vocabulary. It does not mean for Luther "accepting," or "deciding for," or "committing oneself to Christ," or any of the misuses this word has received. Faith is *perfect passivity* for Luther—being done unto by God, or simply *suffering* God. It is literally being put to death as a sinner and raised

as a saint, which is decidedly God's own act through preached words. This is a teaching that Plato and Aristotle did not know.

But Luther would be more dramatic yet, for in the same little autobiography he noted that so far everything could have been learned from the great theologian Augustine if anyone bothered to listen to him. Nevertheless, there remained an "imperfection" in Augustine. God's gift of righteousness was still considered by Augustine to be something of one's own and had to be used and improved upon if the final judgment by God was still to be positive. Even the great Augustine kept thinking of righteousness as something *I* have, or at least some*thing* God has that I *participate* in. In other words, Augustine could not quite think of this righteousness as anything other than a new form of the old law, changing the person for the better and moving him or her toward the goal of complete and perfect righteousness. Augustine could never quite shake the myth of a free human will that never dies, even when he had to face Pelagians who made free will the hallmark of righteousness and God's good creation. Luther was about to remove that imperfection by rejecting free will before God. That required walking a different road in Scripture and a big hammer, wielded by God.

CHAPTER FOUR

The Simple Sense of Scripture: Letter and Spirit

The letter kills, but the Spirit gives life.

(2 Corinthians 3:6)

The reason Luther's struggle with Paul did not merely begin another school of thought under the generous and tolerant umbrella of the pope began with another little word—"trope." A trope in Latin or in Greek was a turn of a phrase, and in books on speech making, such as Quintillian's, it was considered an ornament—like grace notes in music. A trope was style rather than substance. So, for example, instead of simply saying "The man was tall," a good phrase-turner could make the dull fact memorable by injecting humor, as Cicero once did: "He bumped his head against the Fabian arch." A tall man indeed, and a nice trope.

Trope came to have particular meaning for theologians by Luther's day who developed a four-level apparatus to get meaning out of the Bible's special "turns of phrase." After all, what do you do with a Bible that is full of stories about God and Israel when you are not Israel? By Luther's day the dominant method was to look for hidden meaning, or allegory. The Holy Spirit was understood to have hidden mysteries in Scripture that were revealed later for Christians. So Scripture was understood first as what God once did among his people Israel (historical) and second what God was promising Christians in signs tucked under the surface of events (mystically, allegorically) such as the exodus or David's kingship. Then church tradition went further yet, teaching Christians to turn the Bible's story around from what *God* once did to ask what *you* are to do. "Trope" was the term used for this "third" meaning of Scripture (tropological): a speech turned around toward *us,* that is, toward our ways of behaving, as Philo liked to say. Whether you were reading about Adam and Eve or the poetry of Solomon you were eventually to ask, What moral act is God asking of me? The answer was the tropological sense of Scripture that taught you how to love. There was a fourth level of interpretation, called anagogical, that concerned future hope and its connection to the church, but hope would have to wait for Luther, until he understood what Scripture demanded of him.

The Old, Twisted Trope

For Christians, then, trope was much more than a turn of phrase. It took up the whole question of anthropology or human morality: What does Scripture say I should do? Luther never discounted this U-turn in understanding Scripture. He was, after all, to become the great champion of the proper application of the pronoun "for you." Nevertheless, he was soon to give an absolutely shocking answer to that moral question in light of what Christ had already done on the cross. What does God require of you in order to be judged right before him? *Nothing at all!* But that bomb thrown into the middle of the Christian theological party has to wait, since we are getting ahead of Luther's own trope or story.

Though this method of interpreting Scripture was positively poetic, for Luther it was like fire burning a hole in his pocket. If the Bible is supposed to teach you what God expects out of you, you had better get this down pat or your goose is cooked. In particular, Luther went right to the root of allegorical interpretation in Paul's second letter to the Corinthians, where Paul distinguished between the letter that kills and the Spirit that gives life (2 Cor. 3:6). Does "letter" there really mean the past history of the Jewish people? Does "Spirit" really mean transcending this visible world spiritually as one rises to God? If so, by what means? By considering what Paul really meant by mystery as the distinction of Spirit and letter (the literal sense of Scripture) and at the same time what tropology demanded of him, the system began to implode for Luther. The church had not taken the place of Israel and improved on its laws by allegorical interpretation, Luther argued. Nor was Spirit the hidden key to unlock the mystery of history, as the method assumed.

Yet people have a gravitational attraction for the trope, not for the simple and clear word of Christ. They want to turn the words of the text to "mean" something according to their own desire to be saved by the law. Tropology may have begun as the tail among Scripture's mysteries, but it was soon wagging the whole dog in actual church life. It was, after all, the basic stuff people wanted to know. What does God expect from me? People come to church to hear from the preacher what they are expected to do and not do. So trope was not a grace note for very long but became the main stuff of sermons. Luther was a man about to be judged, about to die (since Paul said that the letter *kills*), and so he naturally wanted to know what that letter of Scripture demanded of him tropologically. Consequently, he turned the whole system of church interpretation on its head, putting the trope first.

Suppose, as Luther did at the time, that exercising the virtue of love was the real thing that God expected from

sinful creatures. How does one ever love enough to please Jesus Christ, the final judge and jury? Luther thought he was applying the nutcracker to Scripture to get its final word on this matter, but he soon found that Scripture was applying its vice to him until the fourfold interpretation of Scripture caved in, and letter and Spirit ceased being *history* (what happened to Israel or the disciples) and *mystery* (what God's plan for all time is) and became instead God's working on sinners called *law* and *gospel*. God was using the very words of Scripture to consign everything of Luther's own under sin—boxing it up and calling it dung, or worse, *rebellion* against God. This assumes that people come to Scripture with myths of their own creation and that the written words must break them. When Luther actually read Scripture he realized that even his best religious activities as a monk were counted as sin. Why would God do this? Is he just a grumpy old man? Does he set us up for a fall, telling us what we must do—love God above all, and our neighbors as ourselves—only to watch us fail and to laugh while we go to hell? Is tropology just a big and mean joke to God? Luther began to sense what was at stake. Once you start down tropology road you eventually get to a dead end: "For God has imprisoned all in disobedience" (Rom. 11:32a) and "the scripture has imprisoned all things under the power of sin" (Gal. 3:22). So here is Luther's conversation with Scripture:

LUTHER: What am I to do?

BIBLE: Love.

LUTHER: What does God do with my very best love efforts?

BIBLE: He assigns them all to the column called "sin."

LUTHER: Is that all there is? Am I done for?

There is a surprising ending to each of those sentences from Scripture, but we are trudging with Luther through the old trope. For now, Luther could go no further, having reached the dead end of tropology road and about to go over the cliff.

Whether the old trope came in the package of the old theology in Luther's day (Thomas Aquinas's *via antica*), or the new theology of people such as Occam or Biel (called *via moderna*), or even Augustine's theology of grace, they all came to the same conclusion about what you need to do. You are on a quest or pilgrimage. God's grace is help on your road to get where the law demands you be.

Unravelling that tightly wound mixture of law and gospel would not only take years for Luther, but it created the great struggle of conscience that Luther called *Anfechtung*. True, Paul says, run your race, but the end of that race for Paul was the final death of his old Adam; it was not seeing God's grand design in a beatific vision of God's whole being and plan for the universe. Running your race got twisted in the church to mean that God set up a distant goal of virtue and provided the means for you to reach it through two gifts: one a created free will and the other the law as a guide. The old trope is all about two things: the free will and the law as guide.

The church began weaving its own story around Scripture in order to make law, free will, and God's grace fit together. To have a God meant to be created from the substance of God's original being. Paradise was to exist in harmony with all things according to God's original order or law. That order was a hierarchy of being extending like steps from God down to the tiniest earthly elements, such as a grain of sand, that exist at a great distance from God. As the story goes, the substance of God's original being was given to humans in a special way in the form of freedom of choice. But humans for some strange reason (perhaps to prove to themselves that they really do have freedom!) immediately chose badly and continue to do so—thus losing their proper place in the world—and so fall out of relationship or union or participation with God's own being. This tragedy means that now human flesh and spirit are all confused about how to get back to their proper place in the universe. Fallen humans must then begin a long journey to climb back up the stairs to take their proper place—but this arduous journey can be completed only with the proper help from God, in particular through the revealed law as a guide. Dante needed a guide both in hell (a righteous pagan) and in purgatory (love herself) to find his way back to paradise! So God's new grace is then the law itself that helps the last remaining part of the old grace found in the little bit of free will that remains.

The secret or mystery of this old story is that grace

means the divine law is designed to help the free will. Law teaches how to overcome temptations of flesh and transcend to the life of spirit. The more you know the law, the clearer your path comes into focus; and the more help given to complete it, the greater the participation in life as you move toward the final goal of rejoining God's original being. Just like the old formula for a good movie—boy gets girl, boy loses girl, boy gets girl back—so it was for Christians to become right before God. You once had righteousness, lost it, and through Christ you start to get it back. This old trope forces you to think of righteousness as a substance that I myself have, that I lose to some degree (though a spark remains), and that I get back to some degree (as measured by the law) until righteousness can be perfected in *myself* by being reintegrated into God's original plan of creation.

That little word "myself" is always the star *dramatis persona* of this story's plot. The law is my friend and lifeline as I make my way through the brambles of earthly lust back to God's original plan for my life. The story speaks, as Luther would say in his famous lecture on Romans, of "quiddities"—stuff you own or have or are getting put back into that is usually called "ontology." It forces the entirety of Scripture to be the allegorical story of a great exodus, not from Egypt to Israel, but tropologically moving from vice to virtue. In the end, you are supposed to find your way back to a hidden God by using the breadcrumbs of the law as your guide.

It is remarkable how many stories can be made to fit this tropological template—from pagan mystery cults and Greek philosophical schools to the whole of the world's religions and including the Bible itself. Plato's picture of your life as a charioteer fits this story. Your soul is like a charioteer with two horses pulling in different directions as

you try to get back to Mount Olympus. Aristotle's picture of a whole oak inside the little acorn can be read this way too. Certainly one might read the story of Adam and Eve according to the one note of law. So losing glory and regaining it by a hard journey became the subplot or shadow story line Luther read, like everyone else, into every part of Scripture. This trope then gave him an answer to his question, What does God want from me? He wants me to strive for righteousness, helped by grace, until I have fulfilled the law in my own person and I fit back into God's big plan for the universe. The problem was that Christ entered back into this picture as judge, who says at the end of the journey, "Well done, good and faithful servant," or who pulls the cord and down you go on the one-way elevator to hell.

The Tropes Changed: The Law, Until Christ

Luther was in mid-fall while he was beating on Paul at this second point: "The letter kills, but the Spirit gives life" (2 Cor. 3:6). What is Scripture saying, or better, doing, to you? It is imprisoning all your "things" under the power of sin (Gal. 3:22a and Rom. 11:32a). The law does not make alive; law is not the goal nor is law the guide to righteousness before God. Law condemns you as guilty even with your best parts. No one is perfect as God is perfect, none at all. Is that all there is?

Thankfully, no. There is more to say. There is a purpose clause that follows God's fearful condemnation of our efforts: "*so that* what was promised through faith in Jesus Christ might be given to those who believe" (Gal. 3:22b), and in Romans 11: "*so that* he may be merciful to all" (v. 32b). For Luther, the tropes changed by taking these two absolutes seriously: All our tropology is sin; God then acts out of sheer mercy so that what was promised to faith in Jesus Christ would in fact be given. The law stands—until Christ—and there it ends.

Salvation is not the progress of a spiritual athlete for whom practice in the law makes perfect. It is not even like a sick person getting well on the medicine of grace, for those pictures of Christian life leave Christ on the sidelines while human free will takes center stage. Such notions leave Christ idle, displacing him by the star of that drama, the free will that dreams of becoming ever more holy under the law. Why then the *cross*? Did Christ come simply to remind people of the law that Moses already gave, or even to give an improved version of the tablets of stone? Is Christ to be patient while you try to solve the puzzle of God's law? The story of Scripture, Luther began to understand, is not how *we* make our way up the mountain by getting grace and

then topping it off with love and works. Scripture is the story of how *God came down to meet us—while we were yet sinners.* Christ is the mover and shaker, the active subject, the star of the show. And when Christ comes the law ends. Luther coined a phrase—*crux sola nostra theologia* (the cross alone is our theology)—and put it in capital letters to stand out boldly as the chief truth he found while lecturing on Psalms for the first time.

Theologians of the Cross

When the stories changed for Luther, everything became different as read out from the cross of Christ rather than the law and free will. Everything depended on God doing two things, not one: destroying and raising up, just as

Hannah first sang (1 Samuel 2) and Mary joined in when she received the promise of bearing the Savior (Luke 1). Consequently, all things had to be shifted from "quiddities," or substances that make a thing what it is, to their relation to God's work in the cross—how they stand *coram deo* (how God sees things) rather than *coram hominibus* (how humans see things). The great exodus or journey for Christians was not from vice to virtue (getting better according to the law, as the great church tradition had it), but moving from virtue to faith, from morality to Christ. Imagine what the church thought of Luther when he concluded that Christ frees us from *virtue*. Even the old pagans never tried that dangerous assertion! Nevertheless, Luther used that change of tropes, the new form of exodus, as his masthead for his great lecture on Romans. "Get ready," he was telling his students, "God is changing the story so that he is the subject for once, and you the object."

In a way that remains shocking to current interpretation theory, Luther eventually asserted that Scripture is clear and interprets itself. Among other places, Luther used the phrase *sui ipsius interpres* (Scripture interprets itself) in his response to the papal bull that excommunicated and damned him to eternal hell. In the end, according to Luther, *you do not interpret Scripture; it interprets you.* The word *understand,* after all, means "to stand under." That is not what modern people think when they come to the Bible and imagine that they stand *over* its texts to "figure them out." God wrestled Luther by the clear words of Scripture and wouldn't let him have his precious myths of free will and partial grace. So while he was pounding on Scripture to know what Paul wanted, God was busy pounding on him to hear the new song with both of its notes: The letter *kills* because you are not righteous by the

law; the Holy Spirit alone *gives life* because it makes faith where you put works demanded by the law. Yet who could deny the conclusion? If Christ were everything then free will would be nothing.

Luther then set about to rid the church of its long-standing preoccupation with a form of Gnosticism (secret knowledge about certain mysteries) that has tried to be rid of the Old Testament by turning Scripture's "law" into something old and Jewish and "gospel" into nothing but better laws. That false step tried to make Christ into a better Moses than the Jews had. It made the church a superior

65

form of the Jewish synagogue. It put final church author-ity in the papal office instead of in Scripture alone. It put law where gospel belonged, and its effect was to bury Jesus Christ under self-righteous motives to keep everyday Christians from becoming immoral. To the contrary, Luther came to assert that Scripture was not hiding mys-teries, nor was the church improving on Moses' laws. Scripture is clear, interprets itself, and so needs no papal office to provide its true meaning. The Scripture must interpret the pope, not vice versa.

For Luther, everything in this life and the next depends on how faith is made in the act of a preacher declaring, "Your sins are forgiven on account of Christ." Those are the simple, clear words of Scripture finally "interpreting" you, the sinner. Whether you are Abraham (who came before Christ) or Luther (who came after), when God gives you a promise, it alone makes you righteous. Your whole life is then in God's hands, and you cling to that word like a drop of water clings to the outside of a pitcher. You don't

spend your life spinning out new myths and tropes of your own liking. Saints of the Old or New Testaments were no longer considered by Luther to be spiritual athletes advancing on virtue, but drops of water hanging on for dear life, or worse. As Jeremiah prophesied, "Is not my word like fire, says the LORD, and like a hammer that breaks a rock in pieces?" (Jer. 23:29). God's big hammer was about to fall on Luther. For that we take up Luther's own experience with penance.

CHAPTER FIVE

For God, to Speak Is to Do: Pastoral Care of Souls

For the promise that he would inherit the world did not come to Abraham or to his descendants through the law but through the righteousness of faith.

(Romans 4:13)

Law and gospel would never be distinguished and Christ truly preached, Luther thought, while pastoral care of sinners was practiced according to the traditional sacrament of penance. Luther experienced penance as his own life-and-death struggle and at the same time as trouble for his parishioners, who got caught up in the practice of buying indulgences. He came to believe that a foreign idea stemming from false tropology had mangled penance as actual forgiveness of sins, so he began one of his writings on "the office of the keys" this way: "The horrible abuse and misunderstanding of the precious keys is one of the greatest plagues which God's wrath has spread over the ungrateful world."[1]

The heart of the way pastors care for souls concerns how they deal with sin and repentance. In Luther's day, both priest and penitent came to be preoccupied with the imaginary inner life of the sinner instead of the announcement that "your sins are forgiven," called absolution. Penance came to be the real stuff of repentance. If a person were truly sorry for sin, then God's forgiveness would certainly follow quickly. So by the time sinners came to a priest and the priest inspected them for signs of true sorrow, it was already too late for the priest to do anything. God had already forgiven or not. The priest was there merely to make God's prior judgment on the matter known so the person could be reassured. The priest remained curiously outside the inner movements of repentance trying to peek into the human heart. For that reason the priest's words came late, after the real stuff of the human heart had already done its work. Priests were cast in a similar role as that of modern therapists who are able to echo back what a patient says but are unable to change the reality by giving forgiveness themselves.

A penance was a penalty, or little sacrifice, that gave to God a partial token to represent the repentance of a whole life. So a prayer or deed was used as a little penalty to diminish any remaining guilt for a person. Though this was meant to relieve people from the burden of guilt, such pastoral malpractice did not cure sin-sick souls. On the con-trary, it increased uncertainty and self-righteousness *at the same time.* If it were not so destructive it would have been a remarkable accomplishment to reinforce despair and pride in one fell swoop! More importantly, as Luther expe-rienced it, penance usurped the priest's authority to announce forgiveness and actually accomplish it. The pro-nouncement "I forgive you" had been emptied of Christ himself as promise, and forgiveness became an external labeling process that at best kept a sick person alive, albeit on life support in the matter of hope.

Baptism and the Development of Penance

Luther was taught in church and monastery that baptism forgave original sin. It righted one's boat in the sea of this sinful world, ridding a person of Adam's inherited sin (probably transmitted through the male seed in inter-course) but leaving its *fomes,* or tinder, behind. At the strike of lust's match, this tinder could reignite and place the sinner back in mortal peril before God. Baptism had been expended getting rid of original sin, and it could be of no further help if one sinned afterward. Subsequent sins had to be addressed by the means of penance, which came to be known by Jerome's description of a second plank or life preserver thrown out to those whose ship had sunk again into sin. By Luther's day, confessing one's sins and having them forgiven by the priest had evolved into a series of steps that would assure a "true" confession as laid out, for example in Peter Lombard's *Sentences*—first *contrition,* second *confession,* and third *satisfaction.* The priest to whom you confessed was there to judge true or false con-trition, hear the enumeration of sins, and apply the proper label in the form of giving or withholding absolution.

71

Words of forgiveness, "I absolve you," were external signs that the substance or inner emotion of sorrow was truly present already in the penitent. A final penalty or satisfaction could be added by the priest who, like a court judge, selected from the appropriate laws to complete the repentance and make people feel like they had paid their debt to society and God. Only then could they go on with their lives and try to "sin no more."

The result of this process was that the law was found fore and aft, and the promise of forgiveness became an external stamp of approval for the process by the local spiritual expert. Words came too late to a process that "really" took place inside the person. That is what it meant to confuse law and gospel in the middle of an actual life for someone who really had sinned and needed forgiveness. Luther experienced a series of basic problems with this process that

destroyed his trust in the church's ability to make spiritual laws and cooked and fried him like a pig on a spit.

The Fruit of Penance: Pride and Uncertainty

The first problem for Luther with penance as a second plank was what we might call psychological. It created false faith (pride) in works of satisfaction that followed the announcement of forgiveness, rather than faith in the promise itself. After all, if a penalty comes after being forgiven, what do you suppose a person will begin trusting as the real act of being forgiven? Putting trust in making satisfaction was simply another form of pride in works. At the same time, strangely enough, penance created uncertainty because contrition was notoriously hard to name. It was, after all, a deeply inner disposition capable of enormous deception for self and others. Christians didn't have to wait for Freud's psychoanalytic theories to recognize the enormous human capacity for self-deception and deception of others that lies between inner feelings and outward appearance. Some people look really sorry and are not. Some people appear unfazed but inside are deeply troubled. How much sorrow at sin was ever enough to be called "real"? Luther found by painful experience that the better you are at doing the law in this way, the greater your uncertainty becomes. The clearer you are about the demands of the law, the more you must reduce the law's unmanageable demand to make it manageable—resulting in a classic double bind. The more you praise the law as God's eternal form of salvation, the more you must deny its limitless demand on you: "Be perfect, therefore, as your heavenly Father is perfect." Instead, you come to say, "Do your best." God can't expect more than that, right?

To keep the penitent from dying outright in the process

73

of repentance, both the self and the priest were pressed into the service of reducing the law's demand to manageable proportions. Priests became experts in casuistry (which penalty belonged with which sin) and upon that rested the hope of the guilty. I suppose it is like going to a diet doctor who knows that even in drastic circumstances one has to begin making small steps to thin down. So it was for pastoral care. The priest began taking the role of a medical doctor doling out prescriptions and therapies to keep a sick patient alive.

Luther observed that when a person is left with the law as the form of God's grace, the tell-tale psychological signs are pride and uncertainty—at the same time. Sinners themselves are actively dumbing down the law's demand so they can feel confident that they have done enough. Forgiving one's enemies or honoring parents cannot

really be demanded in every single instance, can it? Aren't there extenuating circumstances when enemies would take our life, or parents are undeserving? So on goes the process of whittling down the law—or, as Luther liked to say, making a "whittled-down God" that we prefer to the real one.

Verbum Reale

But an even greater problem in penance showed itself to Luther. He began to see in his own practice of asking and giving forgiveness that the real reason for the sacrament of penance had essentially disappeared. The purpose of the sacrament of penance is to give God's own forgiveness as a promise to people who really need it because the law's demand is crushing them. But instead of being a *forgiver*, the priest had become a *judge*. The priest judged if contrition were true; he then doled out manageable portions of law to keep the patient (already on life support) alive as a doer of the law. A tangle of law and gospel came out in the form of a subjunctive prayer in which the priest hoped to God his judgment was right. So the priest became the judge and the penitent a defendant. When the priest spoke, it was necessarily a word of law alone—this penance applied to that sin as an act of catholic equity that made "mercy" or "grace" into lighter penalties than sinners actually deserved. The church's priest then ran around the battlefield putting bandages on mortal wounds, offered a wish and a prayer, and sent people on to stand trial before the final judge.

Luther realized that this way of giving pastoral care failed to distinguish law and gospel. Consequently, the priest's word of judgment was first a mere label put on the person's prior, inner movement of the will. Then the priest's word became an artificially limited accusation, like radiation for a cancer patient, meant to get sinners as close to death as possible without actually killing their free will. Luther began to see in Scripture that God's word is not so limited and dependent upon the sinner's last remaining bits of free will. When God speaks a word it is "sharper than a two-edged sword" (Heb. 4:12) and "will not return to him empty, accomplishing its purpose" (Isa. 55:11). Unlike human words that are often just hot air, God's words actually accomplish things on earth. Yet even for Augustine, words were external to real things. Words were a weak stand-in for something else considered "substantial" or "real." They either were mere labels for things in themselves that could be switched at will (you could call your pet a "dog" or "puppy" and refer to the same animal), or words were signs that pointed away from themselves to real things that resided elsewhere. A sign pointing to falling rock is not an actual falling rock. Take your pick, *exchangeable labels* or *external pointers* to an absent thing, either way the word of promise became external to the real stuff of repentance. The priest's words labeled, or merely pointed at, the real thing that was happening inside a penitent. Luther began to see that he had been sold a bill of goods by philosophy and church—that something "inner" was the real thing, and words hovered outside a penitent like marsh gas.

Luther eventually rejected all this misuse of words as both unbiblical and a pastoral malpractice. The real matter in the sacrament of penance was not to talk about sin but to do something about it. It was not to theorize about sin but to change the world of sinners. God's word as used in Scripture was not the weak sister of your own inner humility but was the thing itself, the reality and truth by which God actually forgets your sin and gives you Christ instead.

Modernity and postmodernity have not caught up to Luther here. Even the odd philosopher who agrees that words sometimes "perform," or get things done rather than merely describe, has not yet scratched the surface of what Luther found.

Luther once lectured rather late in his life on the second psalm. That psalm is frightening when it says about the affairs of this world, "He who sits in the heavens laughs; the LORD has them in derision" (v. 4). Who, in the moment of contrition or in the hour of death, can bear that? Does God laugh while we perish? But then Luther noted that everything changes when God leaves off laughing and *speaks:*

But what or in what manner will He speak? Here we must observe the Hebrew way of expression. For when Scripture says that God speaks, it understands a word related to a real thing or action (*verbum reale*), not just a sound, as ours is. . . . And when He speaks, the mountains tremble, kingdoms are scattered, then indeed the whole earth is moved. That is a language different from ours. When the sun rises, when the sun sets, God speaks. When the fruits grow in size, when human beings are born, God speaks. Accordingly the words of God are not empty air, but things very great and wonderful, which we see with our eyes and feel with our hands. For when, according to Moses (Genesis 1), the Lord said, "Let there be a sun, let there be a moon, let the earth bring forth trees," etc., as soon as He said it, it was done. . . . For as the Greek poets have Homer and the Latin poets have Virgil, whose style they imitate, so the holy Prophets have learned from Moses to speak correctly of the acts of God. For they saw that in the case of God *to speak is to do and the word is the deed.* (Italics added.)[2]

Once this *verbum reale,* a real word that does what it says, broke in on Luther, theology and the church could not remain the same. The split between theory and practice, idea and things was transgressed. The priests' words were not describing or judging but altering the universe and changing the course of history. God was not only some prime mover but a sustainer who creates moment by moment. Then again, God was not only a sustainer but a perpetual *interferer.* Though God laughs in the heavens, hidden from sight, he speaks so as to be "felt on earth," as Luther put it. The fulcrum from which the entire earth is to be leveraged and evil defeated is God's own word of promise. Never mind that a spoken word appears as the weakest, most ethereal thing on earth; it is God's tool (mask) to make sinners righteous and defeat death itself.

For Luther then, a priest is not finally a judge but a proclaiming ambassador of Christ who has been authorized to forgive sin here and now. When a priest declares forgiveness to a real sinner, it is according to Christ's own promise: "Whoever listens to you listens to me" (Luke 10:16). Christ's word is no add-on to real things already existing, as if Christ's were merely one more point of view or he was one more creator of a philosophy or religion. Christ is *the* word, and the word was not only with God from the beginning but *is* God (John 1). If that is the case, then if Christ ever spoke a new word it would be no less than a new creation. In the sacrament of penance, Christ not only was the word through whom all things were once made but is the creator of all things new because he has been raised from the dead and is Lord of a new spiritual kingdom. Thus, if Christ chooses to raise the dead by a simple declaration—"Lazarus arise!"—then so it is. For God, "to speak is to do." Lazarus did not come out of the grave because he got his free will in motion to choose resurrection; it was because he received an external command from God's word, which does what it says.

There is no metaphysical distance between what God says and what is. Luther finally understood that new creation by God's word is what should be happening in the sacrament of penance. The priest must actually accomplish forgiveness for an actual sinner by declaring the promise: "On account of Christ, I declare the entire forgiveness of your sins." Otherwise, the church merely sells its divine inheritance for pottage and the world cannot tell the difference between a therapist and priest, except that one is cheaper.

An Idle Christ

Luther then unearthed a third great problem with penance. If it first produced self-righteousness and despair, and second substituted doling out penalties for the true absolution, then third and most damning, it made Christ superfluous. Because the priest had been put in the impossible position of judging inner dispositions, then he could only offer a word of forgiveness with a big "maybe" written in large letters over the whole thing. Luther actually recorded one of the current monastic forms of absolution in his later lecture on Galatians so that "posterity may understand how infinite and unspeakable the abomination of the papal kingdom was":

> May the merit of the suffering of our Lord Jesus Christ, of Blessed and Ever Virgin Mary, and of all the saints; the merit of your order; the burden of your order; the humility of your confession; the contrition of your heart; the good works that you have done and will do for the love of our Lord Jesus Christ—may all this be granted to you for the forgiveness of your sins, for the growth of merit and grace, and for the reward of eternal life. Amen.[3]

You do hear Christ named in that "absolution," but only in the form of a wish dependent on what *you* do. Luther finally saw the christological problem in the way the church was practicing its penance: "Christ is completely idle here," he concluded.

It is amazing to think that in the Christian church the whole notion of forgiveness could actually reach the point where Christ was extrinsic—outside the real matter of how forgiving got done. The free will and the law had become the only indispensable truths of this theological system.

Christ became an idler watching to see if someone repenting fulfilled the proper conditions for righteousness by law. Sometimes Christ was described as a spur to the will by providing an example—What would Jesus do? But as Luther repeatedly observed, "One must not make Christ a law professor, as the pope has done."[4]

The tell-tale sign of setting up an idle Christ in theology is not that Christ never gets mentioned, but two of the most basic words of the gospel are emptied of meaning, namely, "justification" and "faith," as in Paul's "a person is justified not by the works of the law but through faith in Jesus Christ" (Gal. 2:16). Justification had become the name for the moral process of the will striving for perfection, and then God's help in that process (call it grace if you like) merely supplied the needed merit for transforming an unrighteous person into a righteous one by the standard of the law. Christ was an add-on. Faith became merely your personal potential, a cup needing to be filled by acts of ordered love (*fides caritate formata*), as the scholastic traditions put it.

But this synthesis of whittled-down law and halfway grace ends up with your will either in the slough of despondency or in the haughty seat of self-righteousness. Such is the basic bipolarity of pious Christians for whom law and gospel remain tangled. And so they swing between depression and pride, with priests going for the ride while struggling to keep the patient alive through penance. Both of those dispositions destroy faith in Christ by putting in his place the renewed human will as the final step to salvation. Yet the apostle Paul put it succinctly: "If justification comes through the law, then Christ died for nothing" (Gal. 2:21). You cannot have it both ways—the law *and* Christ. Moreover, Christ is in fact not idle. He won't stand for it. He interferes. Jesus Christ got loose, even from death! Christ came into this world and messed up the system of salvation

that the church was offering through penance. Christ raised from the dead is Christ unbound, even by the law or by a sinner's vain attempts to tame the law.

If that is the case, then what will you do when Christ comes to you by the mere little words of a preacher who declares the actual forgiveness of your sins? Luther put it bluntly in a Pentecost sermon on John 3:16: "The world is not judged because it did not keep what God commanded through Moses. This is the judgment: it does not want the Son! . . . Other sins are mere fleabites in comparison like when my kids, Hans and Lena go poop in the corner and we laugh. Faith does the same thing, it overcomes the stink of our own excrement before God."[5]

Luther's New *Seelsorge*, or Cure of Souls

All of Luther's theology is finally pastoral cure of souls, and that amounts to how you go about giving Christ to people who do not want him. Why do people not want Jesus' own righteousness as a gift? Because they do not want to die. Instead, they perpetuate the dream that they can live before an angry God by getting better at doing the law with a little help from God's grace. Luther believed a whole edifice built on this theory of bad pastoral care had to be torn down. Priests were not mediators between sinners and God, offering appeasing sacrifices or saying a prayer. Christ alone was the mediator between the angry God and a sinner. But priests should be "means" in the opposite direction, because it was their job to absolve sinners and get forgiveness done. In order for that to happen, Luther liked to stiffen the spine of priestly absolvers with the example of John the Baptist. Honest-to-goodness sinners need John's simple sermon, "Repent!"—not just a bit, but as Luther put it in his famous ninety-five theses, God demands one's *whole life* to make a complete turn. Sinners need no less than a whole new life. Jeremiah said you need a new *heart* (Jer. 31:33). You need to be a whole new person, not merely have a new inner resolve. The preacher must not allow *anyone* to be right before God by the law in any respect. Give no false escape. Allow no fiction. No more dumbing down the law. The law must stand out in its complete accusation against whole sinners, not just their lower parts but especially their best and highest (that includes their free will). The wages of sin is death. Such a judgment is not made because of a sinner's contrition but because Jesus Christ was crucified by law-abiding people.

Such a sermon was only possible when Christ had actually arrived. Then the finality of the law could be uttered and a new word could be declared. Luther liked to say (especially in Advent sermons) that the second part of John the Baptist's sermon must bring back "the long, pointing finger" that takes the sinner from himself or herself "over there" to Christ, "the One from whose fullness we all must receive grace upon grace and without whom no human being can be justified before God."[6] "Behold the lamb of God!" is the new, second word (or gospel) of John's sermon. When the gospel arrives the law must be shut up in the voice of the conscience where only Christ is allowed to speak. From Christ's mouth come absolute promises: "Repent, and believe in the gospel" (Mark 1:15).

It began to dawn on Luther that repentance as revealed in Christ was not just feeling sorrow, receiving penance, and completing the works of the law; it was the most radical change possible. Repentance was putting the old sinner to death and raising up the dead to new life, having "been born of God." But that, in turn, unseats the penitent's own self as the active subject of repentance *and* as the continually existing object of God's help. It is not as if the sinner is undergoing a process of having sin removed while he or she remains basically the same person. Instead of having *sin* removed from the person, Luther began to say, it was the *person* being removed from sin—being put to death and raised. The sinner is the one acted upon, not the one doing the acting.

Once the edifice of the old form of repentance tumbled, Luther found that Christ came back to the center of the priest's announcement. Baptism also became first and always the source of the whole Christian life, never to be "used up" in original sin or become useless for the sin that followed in a person's life. In this sacrament Christ becomes the active one, the one whose cross works the final, true repentance and whose promise has power unlike anything the law demands. Sin is truly forgiven only by the power of the word of promise. So Luther taught in his *Small Catechism* that baptism "brings about forgiveness of

sins, redeems from death and the devil, and gives eternal salvation to all who believe it, *as the words and promise of God declare.*"

Luther began to experience a Christ broken out of the bubble of eternal law itself. God's "absolute freedom" that the nominalists only speculated about actually entered into Luther's very life and seized him. You can imagine that if Prometheus unbound was a problem for business as usual on earth, then Christ unbound, resurrected from the dead and invading the world's darkness, was the beginning of the end of what the world holds sacred. Beyond the law, Christ alone is your righteousness, not through any work but simply through trust in God's declared words and promises.

Already in 1519, as the *verbum reale* was sinking in for Luther, he turned the sacrament of penance around: "[T]he priest does no more than to speak a word, and the sacrament is already there."[7] That means priests have a powerful promise to give, authorized by Christ himself: "I will give you the keys of the kingdom of heaven, and whatever you bind on earth will be bound in heaven, and whatever you loose on earth will be loosed in heaven" (Matt. 16:19). The church called this the "office of the keys." The absolution is the reason for the sacrament, and it is accomplished by applying Christ's promise to a dying sinner.

So a new pastoral care was born in Luther's discovery. There must be a repentance that is a complete change of the whole person. That could only be accomplished by having the old Adam put to death and a new creature arise, and this is not possible for persons to drum up within themselves.

For that reason, even when he removed penance from lists of sacraments, Luther did so only because he had moved the office of the keys and the forgiveness of sins to the center of all the preacher does and of the Christian life itself. The preached word itself became sacrament. There at the center of pastoral work the power of the papacy emanating from its presumed authority to "command" or "forbid" (especially *inside* the Christian conscience) came to an end. When Christ rules in the heart another voice rings in the inner ear: "You are mine; I have claimed you." The preacher thus became what some have called "the local forgiveness person." God's word in Christ does exactly what it says, creating out of nothing.

Luther was in the process of discovering the difference between promise and penance just like that in the story of

Jesus healing twelve lepers and then sending them to the temple priest for public recognition that the deed had been done. Which was the greater power—to approve a healing, or to heal? To change the world, or merely acknowledge that it had already been changed?

CHAPTER SIX

What Theology Is About:
I, the Sinner; God the Justifier

For in hope we were saved. Now hope that is seen is not hope. For who hopes for what is seen? But if we hope for what we do not see, we wait for it with patience.

(Romans 8:24–25)

For a time, the people of the modern world were not very interested in God as a being different from themselves. Of course, two things are still not to be discussed at a polite party: politics and religion. Being an atheist was just part of growing up, especially once you found yourself in college. But as the saying goes, there are no atheists in foxholes. A world war that seemed unthinkable was followed by a second that unleashed *en masse* the kind of violence only glimpsed at the French Revolution—where whole peoples were scapegoated and a new term was coined: *genocide.* Human "progress" suddenly regressed, and thinkers of all sorts were in a crisis. Martin Luther, who had been largely forgotten since the sixteenth century, suddenly had a new audience. Luther's works were being assembled and edited in the late nineteenth century, prompting a "Luther renaissance," but it wasn't until theologians needed someone to explain how human freedom and unprecedented use of scientific reason had allowed and fostered atrocities that a theologian of the cross began to be heard again.

Luther cannot be made into a hero; indeed, he is still often summarily blamed for this very problem of genocide in the Second World War, once having said that the burning of synagogues by state authorities would be better than public blasphemy of Christ—a blasphemy he dubiously attributed to Jews, as most Christians did. Nevertheless, despite his own sin, he recognized something that had been forgotten about Scripture and our lives: There are no atheists *period* because there are o*nly* foxholes here on earth (Isa. 42:22: "all of them are trapped in holes"). Luther dealt with God because he had to, not because it was interesting or required for a well-rounded education.

Luther once had a daughter who died in his arms. His grief broke him, since he had no other God to pray to than the one who took his child. He was not interested in nice hair-splitting explanations of this event, such as that God didn't want his child's death or had nothing to do with it, or couldn't change it even if he wanted to. In fact, Luther understood that trusting God only increased the problem of having a God, so that he commonly quoted Psalm 116: "I believed, therefore I was greatly afflicted" (au. trans.). If life's main goal is temporarily to minimize problems by hoping they go away, then it is better not to believe in Jesus Christ.

One doesn't do theology in an armchair (despite the title of this book), though an armchair is a fine place to read. One *suffers*, is done unto—then theology, good or bad, will come out. Usually what comes out is pretty bad. Everybody has "a philosophy of life" and is more than willing to unload when someone is listening. How will you ever decide whether you really should have been a Buddhist, or if Scientology is really more your thing? If

Protestants or Roman Catholics are better off on the last day? If you should really be an atheist or create your own religion? But Luther's theology doesn't start in the typical way, with your personal philosophy or culture's large and historic traditions—even one as important as Christendom itself.

For that reason, Luther liked to scoff at the attempts of scholastics to summarize everything known to theology, such as Thomas Aquinas in his *Summa Theologiae*. Luther countered by saying that true theology has a very small *summa* in two simple parts—"I, the sinner" and "God, the justifier." Theology is to magnify those two matters exclusively. Like a biologist looking through a microscope, when theologians speak of humans they use God's word of law to magnify the sinner, who otherwise has a habit of escaping notice. In a similar way, when theologians speak of God they learn by hard experience to turn from endless discussions about "the mind of God" and to isolate the heart of God in Jesus Christ. They magnify God, *the justifier and savior*. Losing either one of them loses contact with reality and enters myth, illusion, projection, wish-fulfillment, or other dreams of the sin-sick soul.

So Luther's theology always begins with God and humans at the same time, but in a wrestling match! That means theology that digs out "the chief part" is an art practiced under duress rather than a collection of facts or a matter of practice that makes perfect. It is something like learning romance. You can practice saying "I love you; will you marry me?" in the mirror, but is it ever different saying it to your lover when your knees are turning to jelly.

Luther thus understood God's call to a theologian quite differently: "A lawyer speaks of man as an owner and master of property and a physician speaks of man as healthy or sick. But a theologian discusses man as sinner."[1]

Know Thyself

The chief mission of an examined life, as Socrates put it, is to "know thyself." Since you are so near yourself this would seem to be a simple matter, but the complications are enormous. How do preachers convince sinners of their sin, and why trouble the world anyway with things it cannot change? It turns out that your own relationship to yourself is a very limited perspective, and what is worse, you can actually deceive yourself. God uses the law to overcome this problem. Luther's conclusion is unequivocal and without exception—to know yourself is to know a sinner. God simply wants faith or trust in his word. But just like a person who is unlucky in love, sinners are notoriously bad at trusting God. How do people come to identify themselves as sinners—through and through?

One of Luther's great contributions to theology is his explanation of the first commandment in his *Large Catechism,* where he takes up the first question of an examined life. There Luther asked a different question than Socrates: What does it mean to *have a god?* Answer: God is that to which you look for all good and help in need. Your own trust, Luther was saying, is the *creatrix divinitatis,* the creator of your divinity. The key to knowing yourself is locating where you put your trust. Luther liked to say that that is what it is like to *have* a God and not *be* one. Your heart can just as easily produce a fake god, or idol, as it can trust that the true God is right. Trust is not a light switch you can

turn on or off. You do not decide one day to trust something or someone. At best you can unearth your trust only well after the fact, and as with Luther, what lies on the other end of your trust is usually a shock. To your eternal amazement, you discover that humans are asses being ridden, beasts of burden, rather than cowboys in the saddle herding wild cattle or charioteers steering toward Mount Olympus.

Like it or not, you are thrown into the world without asking to be born and have to place your trust somewhere. Luther understood from his own experience that God is dead-set on revealing your trust to you. When God's preacher reveals a person it is unsettling, especially for people who are used to looking at their reflection in the pond like Narcissus and falling in love. Not only are humans "trusters" by nature, but they are terrible judges of character and frightened into putting their trust in the wrong people, places, and things. We are like bad serial daters looking for love but falling for the wrong kind of man or woman, suckers for what looks slick and whoever heaps us with false praise. Then we wake up one day and wonder how we got stuck with such a mess. Luther calls this endless search for the next god the result of bad theology, an inveterate taste for "glory." It is a fiction that casts its own will as the main actor in life, whom God helps either at the beginning or the end with a little "grace."

This habit of sinners puts God in a hard place. You can commiserate if you have ever tried to get someone to love you who really loves another. Yet matters of trust are even harder than love, since trust gives over its *entire future* to another. You should be thankful that God not only wants to reveal your foolishness for trusting the wrong one but has another goal that is God's "proper" work. God has found a way to get your trust, though it costs him much. Luther called this the way of the "cross."

Once you have latched onto a false hope, how does God get you to know yourself? He introduces himself to you, repeatedly. For God it must be like living with someone whose memory is going; it would be comical were it not so deadly that God has to keep saying to his own, "I am the LORD your God, who brought you out of the land of Egypt, out of the house of slavery; you shall have no other gods before me" (Exod. 20:2).

Like it or not, what God thinks of you determines where you "stand" in the universe. If you think about it, this is not so unusual. Many people spend their entire lives trying to get over parents who seem not to like them. Is it surprising to think you might trouble yourself about how the God who calls himself Jealous sees you—even if you decide there is nothing out there but the cool, icy void of space? One key aspect of what Luther did with the first commandment was to think relationally as the first step to revealing one's trust. That means he considers not what things are in themselves (quiddities, or substances), but how two or more things are related. But it goes further. Luther began to learn that what really makes us who we are is not the past and where we came from, but the future and where we are going. The real stuff of your life is determined by what you *hope* for—or better yet, *whom* you put your hope in.

Learning to Hear the Creature Waiting

In the forest a birdwatcher learns to listen for birds more than to watch them. A therapist learns to ignore patient projections and to listen for the true source of pain. A theologian must quit describing and defending God against charges of evil and learn to hear the creature waiting. Luther said he learned to think like that from the apostle

Paul, especially from the letter to the Romans:

> The apostle philosophizes and thinks about the
> things of the world in another way than the philoso-
> phers and metaphysicians do. . . . For the philoso-
> phers are so deeply engaged in studying the *present*
> state of things that they explore only what and of
> what kind they are, but the apostle turns our atten-
> tion . . . to what they *will be*. . . . But using a new and
> strange theological word, he speaks of "the expecta-
> tion of the creature." By virtue of the fact that his
> soul has *the power of hearing the creature waiting,* he
> no longer directs his inquiry toward the creature as
> such but to what it waits for.[2]

97

Luther was ever the pastor concerned about curing souls, and so he thought the theological art must quit wasting time on inane arguments about substances—things in themselves. If you want to get to the real thing regarding souls and consciences, learn to "hear the creature waiting"! Luther took an observation from Augustine that goes back even to students of Plato, but then Luther made an exciting change:

> As Blessed Augustine puts its: "*Anima plus est, ubi amat, quam ubi animat*" (The soul is more where it loves than where it lives). . . . Love changes the lover into the beloved.[3]

Nice play on words, but what does it mean? We are not things or substances that sit in ourselves, or souls with no real existence until we act on our potential in pursuit of a goal. We are relations of love. When we love, an exchange takes place in which we give ourselves over to another, hopefully to get ourselves back in a new way as one who not only *loves* but *is loved* ("lover" becomes "beloved" by loving). Do you know people whose love is not returned? That is not real loving because the "lover" never gets changed into the "beloved." Augustine likely means even more than that. True love can *change* others and the self. Yet that is a risky prospect, especially if you marry with the expectation that you can mold your spouse into someone appealing. Too many people have given their hearts and had them trampled on, or do the trampling, and it only gets worse with time and repetition.

Luther made a change in Augustine's phrase because he realized that the apostle Paul puts it differently: "We are saved by *hope* [not by *love*]" (Rom. 8:24–25, au. trans.). Luther does a nice play on the words of Augustine: "And

thus what is hoped for and the hoping person *become one* through tense hoping."[4] Where Augustine says "love," Luther says "hope." So what? Well, everything is shifted by Luther from the present to the future, from love to hope, and the real matter of who you are and what God thinks of you boils down to the matter of faith. Most importantly, this switches directions from what love aims at to what one waits for in hope. The lover pursues; the hoper waits. In whom do you trust? Trust does not come out of thin air but depends upon the words of promise that break in and change your normal course of events. Trust depends upon another to arrive.

You have no doubt heard people say that when they were not expecting it they *fell* in love—as if it were something they couldn't control but wouldn't change for the world. Luther began to realize that hope is not a goal you set or a choice among various options you make but something you receive—I *fell* in hope, or better, *heard* a promise that changed everything. Sometimes theologians call this "eschatological." That is a way of describing what it means to be waiting for the *final* truth. Whatever or whomever you put your trust in, that is who you *become* "through tense hoping." This faith of yours alone will either justify or condemn you; it will either make you disturbed and lost or comfortable and at home in the world with God and others. Such faith is out of your hands; you wait and hope to receive it.

What You Trust Is Who You Become

We humans usually never abandon the game of comparing what we love with what others love. After all, you are always your own best expert when it comes to what you love. No one can tell you better than yourself what food you want, when you "feel the chemistry" with another, whether you like Picasso or Andy Warhol, and so on. Long ago, when I asked people how you know when you're in love, they just turned me back to myself: "Follow your heart," they said, "you'll just know." Finally they asked, "Does she make you happy?" They are largely right. Love is relative. Who can account for taste? It's all a matter of what you like. Even in college classes of great learning we often get no further than comparing tastes and observing that everyone has a unique perspective. True enough, but when you press to the deeper matter of your *hope* then you are your own worst enemy.

Luther was aware that we have endless ways to fool ourselves into false hopes, especially when we have a dog in the race, as they say. That is, when trust is realized as a life-and-death matter, you want to assure yourself that somehow, somewhere, someway you will not really die. Have you ever tried to convince a friend that he or she is in a bad relationship? Good luck. It is nearly impossible to break through when someone has determined to believe a lie. Now increase that problem a thousandfold to sense what it is like when everyone is out to deny the truth that he or she is heading quickly toward death. Try convincing people, as Tolstoy did in his story of Ivan Illyich, that death comes not only to others but to themselves.

True hope, the kind of trust that will not let you down in the end, will have to go against what your eyes have become accustomed to loving. You are addicted to placing your hope in whatever appeals to you, and then love and hope get terribly entangled. In that case, making the proper distinction in order to get hope right is very hard. You fall in love with what your eyes see, and that is only the surface stuff—the slick, glittery, momentary appeal of a thing. Or what is even more dangerous, you start loving your highest morals, goals, and ideals. "Set your goals." "Never give up." "Don't let anyone take away your dreams." Those are all slogans meant to prop up the world's faltering hopes in dying gods. Luther called all that "glory." People do not want hope; they want good stuff *now* and plenty of it. Money, fame, or rewards for good behavior are the commonest little gods around. Perhaps you have seen "glory" theology in action in a con artist boyfriend or girlfriend who says something like, "I just don't feel the chemistry between you and me anymore." Humans are glory addicts. You have to "feel the chemistry" or the relationship is off. Hope placed there, in what you already love, is doomed.

Luther began to hear in Scripture's message of Jesus Christ that *true* hope opposes what you want or love. The true God has come down to meet us here on earth—so far down that he was killed by glory-seeking theologians. But how can Jesus' cross become our hope? No one can love this symbol of capital punishment and of God's own curse, can she? By definition hope is not seen; it is something we wait for. But more yet, true hope belongs where we can find no love, no chemistry of our own—in fact, we are scandalized and appalled by Jesus Christ and what happened to him ("he had . . . nothing in his appearance that we should desire him," Isa. 53:2).

Nothing is more vigorously avoided in this world than

Jesus Christ's murder by all. No one can love the cross no matter how many pretty necklaces display its symbol. But can your *hope* be put there? Can Jesus' cross be the very thing that you have waited for all your life? Can it be that in the cross God has found a way to stop you from chasing other hopes and dreams, bad lovers and all, and plant you where you belong in this old world? Is Christ's ugly cross the very thing that will finally get you to belt out the old blues song with Etta James: "At last!—my love has come along"?

If Luther and the apostle are right, you become what you hope for. And the cross of Jesus Christ doesn't look very promising to people who are trying to "move up" in the love department. How can hope wait tensely, like a wound spring, for something as dreary and negative as Jesus, killed? Therein lies the tale of "I, the sinner" revealed by God's law.

CHAPTER SEVEN

Bound and Accused:
Human Will and the Law

Through the law comes the knowledge of sin.
(Romans 3:20)

Luther learned through painful experience that God is a creator who likes things. In direct contradiction, spirituality as humans fancy it is the escape from things. Religion constantly teaches you to run out of the world to find your god; meanwhile God comes to us through "means," or created things. Luther knew this was not pantheism; it was

God using what Luther called "masks" so that his creatures might fear and love him rather than fear and flee him. In fact, God, the Father Almighty, gives himself to his creatures along with the things that were made—withholding nothing. Sin, however, makes the Father's giving into hiding. Without knowing this you might find it strange that Luther paused in his last great Bible lecture on Genesis (1535) to say that of all the philosophies and religions of the world, it is the "anthropomorphists" (from so-called primitive or animistic religions) who are closest to the truth. They set up handmade images such as totems or statues and believe they find God there. Luther thought that they were not so far off as the dreamers who set up metaphysical "ideas" and "rituals" and "methods" of heightening spirituality in the vain attempt to help transcend our low and mean estate on earth. The only thing missing in anthropomorphic religion is a clear and specific word of promise to go with the totem pole, for the created things too easily become worshiped in themselves instead of being God's self-giving masks.

Hide-and-Seek

God is never naked for humans but gives himself "clothed" in created things, particularly through human words. In one limited way this love for clothes made God vulnerable. Though humans cannot possibly overcome the naked, all-powerful predestinating God of fate and chance (like Oedipus), they *can* trample all over the Holy Spirit, who comes in things. Humans always suspect God hides behind words and things, and so they decide to manipulate the situation. Adam and Eve were deluded into thinking that if they could find God *behind* masks of creation, they could be "like God" themselves. But God won't stop being God even if humans trample on him in his words, works, and things of earth. No wonder that Luther believed creation was the last and hardest of all the Christian teachings to grasp. Nothing is harder to trust than that God will provide all that is needed for life "day by day," as Luther says in the *Small Catechism*. Our trust is so small that we cannot even be confident that we will have food for tomorrow's table, to say nothing of what it would mean to be made right with God by faith.

Instead, sinners invent their own words to comfort themselves, such as "God helps those who help themselves." Just as the sailors on Jonah's wind-tossed ship, humans pray to any god they can imagine for help; "misfortune makes many gods," Luther liked to say. Humans insist on believing that God hides from them *behind* created things, and consequently they wonder if God is not holding back the very best life for himself—including what it must be like to *be* a god rather than *have* a god. This way of seeing your relation to God and the purpose of life imitates the children's game hide-and-seek. God hides; we seek.

Luther was convinced that God was going about exactly the reverse of this game. God, who is justice, holiness, love, and goodness in his own being, seeks to be those things outside the inner triune life (Father, Son, and Holy Spirit) in his words on earth. Another way of putting this is that God is everyone's creator, but those to whom God has given his words have an advantage over others. God chose his people Israel by giving them his words through Abraham and Sarah, the patriarchs and prophets, until finally the time was right for the Son to be sent among his people Israel. Paul called this "the advantage" of being Jewish, like himself (Rom. 3). Everyone else on earth must deal with God without words—as a silent fate and frivolous chance. For most people this is too much to stomach. Perhaps you

107

can feel yourself recoiling from a God who chooses some and not others, decides and destines, and so God's free giving to the undeserving (justification by faith alone) becomes the very occasion for being offended: "If God is like that, I'll find another god, or be a god myself." "Bon voyage," Luther would respond, as he did at the end of his great work *The Bondage of the Will*. At that point we part company and I can only wish you the best of "luck." Luther tried that very trip himself by raising the monk's vow above God's own self-giving words and came crashing back to earth like Icarus with his wax wings.

Peeping Toms and Inventors of Words

From Adam and Eve to the present moment, sinners are defined by seeking better words from God than they already have. Gentiles are the real beggars here, waiting for scraps from the table of the Jews. When Christ himself is the *only* way that non-Jews are "grafted" to the vine or chosen to receive God's words, their opposition unfolds in the form of hide-and-seek. They imagine God is hiding his better stuff and enticing them to seek higher and farther. Perhaps it is, they begin to hope, that everyone who is at least trying to be religious will end up at the top of a very great spiritual mountain and find that God is not revealed only in Christ or any other particular religion but that God is the Great Rewarder who saves all that make the good-faith effort to find truth. God hides; we seek. We seek; God rewards. From this basic myth and game, humans begin creating their own form of worship that they think is more suitable for their own sensibilities. It is not hard to believe that God is denigrated and dirtied by particularities of history, people, and things of the world, and so a better God would be one stripped naked who

does not speak or wrestle or come down so far into the muck of this world that his skin smokes. So the cry goes up, "Give me a God I can be proud of, like a pure idea or a transcendent goal!" Once that happens humans are on a mission for more than self-knowledge; they want recognition that they are right and have risen above particular places, times, and cultures. They do not want to smell of particularity and parochialism. They are bound and determined to be like God, knowing the difference between good and evil, believing in their own power to believe, becoming the ground of their own existence without the need to depend on God for every little thing, and so not eternally bound to God by trust in specific promises. They come to think they want God "straight up," with no words or fruit trees or bodies or baptisms of water and testaments given in words, wine, and bread—and no Jews. But for Luther this is all false spirituality that stands outside God's house trying to peer through the windows and catch God with his clothes off. Yet there is nothing more dangerous than a religious peeping Tom.

Humans want God naked and without words or created "things," since those seem to limit and divide people and so seem less "spiritual" by being culturally and historically determined. The underlying reason for false spirituality is revulsion at a God who chooses some for his words, leaving the mass of humanity apparently unchosen. Would God really make me wait for a preacher, and if one is somehow sent then hang all hope for this life and the next on some pasty messenger offering the one man Jesus Christ? The narrowness and unpredictability of that mercy seems preposterous. Luther loved quoting Ovid: "Oft I am moved to think there are no gods!"

Sinners do not like *this* God and instead set about creating a better ideal—a God that allows them room to fill in the blank of divinity with more appropriate subject matter to meet their own needs. Is it any surprise that God's total makeover always comes out looking like your own idealized self? To make God over in your own image, however, one great hurdle must be leaped. God's specific, historical, mediated (given) words must be set aside for other words of your own making. So the serpent opens the door for Eve to play hide-and-seek by asking, "Did God say . . . ?" (Gen. 3:1). In Eve's case the new words themselves were suggested by the crafty serpent: "You will not die; for God knows that when you eat of it your eyes will be opened, and you will be like God, knowing good and evil." Therein lies the recipe for all sin:

- First, receive a word from God: "Eat from all the trees except one." Then act mystified or offended by it: "Why did God say . . . ?"

- Second, imagine God is hiding the best from you, and try finding better words: "God can't really mean you'll die. . . ."

- Third, accomplish the great feat of believing in your own power to believe, as if that power were more trustworthy than the Holy Spirit's words given by the preacher.

- Fourth, behold! You have become your own God who determines his or her own "good and evil."

Original sin is this very sin that entered the world, as Paul puts it, "through one man" (Rom. 5:12), but is repeated in endless variations: Jesus cannot really mean "Take and eat, for this is my body," or "You have not chosen me, I have chosen you," or "Your sins are forgiven," can he? That would seem to make him the only salvation and take away my part to play—and I refuse to be ignored! But Luther believed God is so angry about this mistrust that he does not wait for you to change your mind but rather drives this evil forward until it comes out for all to see.

God Hardened Pharaoh's Heart

In the fall of 1524, the Catholic humanist Desiderius Erasmus had had enough of Luther. He suggested they debate the role of the free will in salvation in order to get Luther's dangerous teaching out in the open. Luther applauded Erasmus for finally attacking the real issue: Do we really have a power called "free choice of the will" by which we can apply ourselves to things leading to eternal salvation or turn away from them? Does God make the ungodly right by killing and making alive, or does God wait for them to cooperate by an act of will guided by the law?

Let's face it, in that debate Erasmus was playing before the home crowd. Inveterate hide-and-seekers always cheer for free will in matters of salvation. Otherwise, it seems that ethics, church law, and the organization of life itself would be overthrown. Without the will and the law, average people would just disregard God's moral precepts and go wild like college kids on spring break. We can't all live on Miami Beach, can we? At one point in the debate, however, Erasmus's debating techniques led him to consider a passage of Scripture that seemed to say the direct opposite: God hardened Pharaoh's heart (Exod. 10:1 and Rom. 9:17, au. trans.). That provided Luther the opportunity for a classic rejoinder: The human will is not free to apply itself to matters of salvation, but in fact is *bound*. Strangely, Luther concluded, a bound will is best, since otherwise we would completely miss Christ while playing hide-and-seek with God.

Did God really harden Pharaoh's heart? Erasmus determined that this word in Scripture must be a trope, a turn of phrase that doesn't mean what it straightforwardly says. Why must it be a trope? Otherwise, it would make God responsible for evil, but even more importantly it would take away Pharaoh's free will to act in accordance with God's demand. Erasmus argued that because the Bible is filled with God's demands there is an implied assumption that the human will can choose for or against God. If there is an *ought* from God, there must be a *can* for humans. Otherwise, what is the point of demanding something from someone who cannot give it? Only when a will would choose rightly or wrongly could God then punish or reward. That, after all, is what makes the world go around, isn't it? Otherwise, God would be liable to no external law himself (unpredictable and predestinating), and humans would be without motivation to behave better. The law cannot help but be God's beneficial teacher for improving the choices of free will by which God's own choices of saving some and damning others would then be reasonable and fair. So when the Bible says that God hardened Pharaoh's heart, it must be a trope that really means that

Pharaoh hardened his *own* heart while God mercifully withheld punishment (i.e., did nothing). Erasmus simply turned the subject and object of the sentence around so that it would fit with his assumption about free will and its secret form of atheism.

Luther thought that this was a good example of original sin at work. It takes God's word and reverses it for its own purpose. This effort always starts by looking good. Erasmus preserved something for the free will; otherwise, humans would be mere puppets in the hands of God and God would then be an evil puppeteer who plays with us for mere entertainment and laughs at our troubles. That conclusion, however, required that Erasmus reverse mercy and wrath and so lose any sense for either of them. For Erasmus, God's mercy came to mean withholding punishment for a time so the free will could choose between good and evil, then God could judge according to the choice made. Mercy had shrunk to God sparing a few moments before the next shoe dropped. That is like telling a criminal the "mercy of the state" is to delay execution for a day—small comfort. Erasmus's rationalism has a clear end point. Mercy eventually becomes God doing nothing. No wonder Luther thought that in Erasmus he had come upon the world's first great, self-indulgent atheist who does not want to have a God but to be one instead.

Wrath also took on a new definition for Erasmus—God acting on his own without regard for the free will and its choices. Luther saw exactly where that argument led— God's mercy became delayed judgment pending the actions of one's free will; God's wrath became any unilateral and unconditional divine act (including God's forgiveness of sinners). What would happen if God just up and forgave one day? For Erasmus that would rob humans of free will, and they would need to deny it. What happens if

114

a preacher comes announcing the forgiveness of sins on account of something Christ did long ago in history? Run for your life, lest such a preacher take your precious free will. Better to preserve faith in your own faith than to be forced against your will to receive a unilateral word from God that you cannot resist—like the terrible word, "I forgive you"! Better to live with reason's own self-made theory than have a God who decides, foreknows, destines, and forgives unconditionally in his Son Jesus Christ. Better to sit on death row with your dignified free will intact than suffer unilateral mercy from a God who loves you without any reason but his own desire for the unlovely! Luther thought this was quite a pretty corner Erasmus painted himself into. Erasmus achieved the great feat of defending himself against God's unconditional forgiveness in a gargantuan pyrrhic victory for free will. Are you sure you want to win, Erasmus, and rid yourself of God's mercy once and for all?

Luther put his finger on the underlying problem with Erasmus's trope idea. Erasmus was unable to make a distinction between God's work through the law and through the gospel. He could only sing monotone while thinking that righteousness comes somehow through a legal relationship to God, who measures all your good and bad deeds. Consequently, reason is forced to put a potentially free will where only the Holy Spirit belongs, because the Holy Spirit is always accusing you of sin and giving everything on earth to Christ: "Therefore just as one man's trespass [i.e., Adam's] led to condemnation for all, so one man's act of righteousness [i.e. Christ's] leads to justification and life for all" (Rom. 5:18).

Who would not be offended when confronted with God's incomprehensible judgments (Rom. 11:33)? But unlike Erasmus, Luther never apologized for God's

omnipotence or "made pretty" with God like most theologians, who try to convince you that divinity is really very nice if you just get to know it. Even when it comes to evil, Luther knew very well that extricating God tidily from responsibility for death and destruction can never establish trust. So in the matter of what makes you right in the end, it will either be your free will or the Holy Spirit—those two do not mix or mutually enhance one another. They are foes who fight to the death regarding your trust.

Pharaoh did not like mercy, especially at his expense. Luther then learned a lesson from Pharaoh: God will not hold back his words of promise—though they directly cause scandal and offense—just because you want to protect your precious "free will." God's ways are not our ways; in the end, this is not oppression but is the only means by which to defeat the death that preoccupies you.

Sparks and Depravities

Luther taught something regarding the basic human problem that is rarely understood. Usually he is lumped together with most Christian and pagan teachers who think that humans are "depraved." Being depraved means that your "love compass" is off. Your will keeps wanting things it shouldn't want, and not desiring the things it should.

As Luther saw it, two kinds of theology fall out from this mistake. On the one hand are those theologians who try to discover some "part" of the human untouched by sin that is still capable of getting love right. When they think they have found such a clean part they call it the "image of God," which was humanity's original state. After sin that image is left in some reduced form like a little "spark" of divinity. Such theologians consider it a praise to the Creator and to the dignity of humans to say that even a little spark of free will remains despite the loss of all other created grace originally bequeathed to humans. Those like Luther who do not imagine a spark of divinity remaining from the old divine flame are considered by the first group as negative regarding human nature.

On the other hand, there are those theologians who relish the notion of sin as "the fall," whose description comes to us especially from Augustine. For them, there is a kind of challenge to outdo each other in demonstrating just how far from God's original goal humans have fallen. Depravity, sometimes even described as "total," would then be a way of measuring just how negative a person can be in describing human ability or potential. This often becomes a curious game to see who can be most dismal about human "nature":

"You think humans are disgusting? Well, I think they are depraved."

"You think humans are depraved? Well, I think they are totally depraved," and so on. As good as sheer negativity feels in relation to the naïveté of the analogical crowd of "sparkers," neither of these includes Luther.

For Luther, humans with all their "capacities," "potentials," or their body and soul are *good* because God said so. That means that human sin is not located especially in *lust*'s pull of bodily desires on the higher faculties of reason and will. Nor is sin located originally in a confused *reason* (not knowing, as Plato tried to have it). Nor is it a flaccid or overly excited *will*. Neither is sin merely located collectively in culture, especially the tendency to value one's own tradition and culture over others or to split into "classes" and dominate whenever your group has power.

But there is a real problem for humans. Humans will not trust God's words as right. We have what you might call a "trust problem." Humans have become uncomfortable in creation as creatures and so seek to go to some other "spiritual" place. Consequently, they leave home and become hide-and-seek drifters who peek in windows looking for God's naked truth. This false faith convinces them that Jesus Christ himself is the source of our problems, not their solution. He is too specific, historical, and goes around indiscriminately forgiving notorious sinners—unilaterally. So the story of Adam's sin goes on, but, if Luther is right, not forever.

Accused and Repented

It is a kind of odd rule, like an inverse proportion, that when one begins theology with the demand of a free will concerning divine things, then one becomes preoccupied with how to limit or bind that freedom lest it get out of hand. That was why Erasmus kept warning that Luther's theology might technically be right about Scripture, but if it got into the wrong hands it would mislead the ignorant into moral chaos. It was true theology but bad public policy.

On the contrary, a theologian such as Luther who began with the assumption that human will is bound before God ends up being preoccupied with enjoying how God frees it. For this reason, true Christian preachers always consider their hearers' bondage before giving Christ's promise, and they fully expect the word to do what it says—kill persons, will and all, and then make them alive. That is a very different kind of preaching than constantly exhorting imaginary free wills to "try again, harder this time!" So Luther concluded that you will have God one way or another— with or without his words. You will deal with God as he is preached, promised, and given in Jesus Christ, or you will have God outside Christ, and that kind of naked God never allows himself to be found.

Luther took the apostle Paul at his word that baptism was where God paid you the wages of sin, which is death, and apart from the law gave the free gift of God that is eternal life in Christ Jesus our Lord (Rom. 6:23). Baptism

is a promise made to you by God, unilaterally, and it orients you entirely to Christ's future as the source of your hope. It makes you a creature waiting for Christ alone to speak as your inner voice: "Whoever believes and is baptized shall be saved." You cannot ever advance beyond that, since there God repents you by taking away your false words and giving you his own unthwartable words. That means baptism is never used up or useful only for "original sin" but not for sins after baptism. It also means that repentance, or "change of direction," is not something for a free will to do, because true repentance does not remove sin from the sinners after baptism—it removes the sinner from sin *in faith itself.* Clinging to the words of God in hope translates you to a new Lord so that your new life is a new kind of *belonging* to the true God in trust.

The difficulty for God is that no one believes naturally in original sin. Sinners have to be taught it, or better, accused of it. Nobody believes they should be blamed for what lies beyond their free will's power. The past generation of Luther interpreters often misunderstood Luther at this point. It became common to suggest that back in Luther's day people were crushed by guilt under an old Roman Church that does not exist anymore. Thus, people no longer worry about an angry God and feel no guilt, so Luther's theology that first preached law and then gospel may have worked once, but no longer. Instead of forgiveness of sins, what people really need now is "meaning" in an otherwise meaningless existence, and law and gospel are no use for that. On the contrary, Luther was always very clear that people in his own day and time didn't believe they sinned originally either, and they had this hunch confirmed by the church when their faults could be bought away or worked off in the form of penance as the final, manageable steps of repentance.

For Luther, the law always accuses because God himself uses it for repentance, and God's law must accuse or it is being misused to cover sin, not reveal it. When the preacher comes to say "Repent," there is nothing left for you to do. It is an announcement that your dream of "free will time" is up. Of course, sinners do not like hearing that their possibilities are impossible. Luther began calling this "the big death," as distinguished from the diminutive death when your body stops, God removes his breath, and others put you in an urn. The world is in the habit of thinking that just about the worst thing that can happen to you is suffering a painful end with a poorly attended funeral and a body burned and spread to the four winds. Luther believed there is much worse, as King David found, who fell under God's wrath and experienced it as an infinitely painful divorce of a creature from his own Creator.

God Repents Sinners

How does God repent someone? The old understanding of repentance was that God used the law as both carrot and stick, penalizing sin and promising rewards for better effort next time. The cause of David's famous plea for mercy in Psalm 51, "Have mercy on me, O God," was thought to be *actual sin*—a willful offense against the law because David let his love become disordered. He supposedly let his higher love for God and the law be overtaken by the lower, bestial form of love by lusting after a beautiful, married woman taking a bath.

Luther began to see that this whole scenario missed what happened to David because it considered sin only by comparing it to the law. "We do not think of sin as lightly as do the pope's theologians, who define sin as 'anything said, done, or thought against the Law of God.' So that sin

121

is simply opposing God's law."[1] One of the consequences of that halfway definition of sin was to miss the finality of God's judgment, and then a series of false distinctions of sins followed that denied the reality of baptism as a death and burial with the crucified Jesus Christ. After all, if the will is going to be the actor in repentance and the law its means, it cannot very well be dead—so thought these "pope's theologians."

Luther simply began with David receiving a word from God and then playing hide-and-seek with it, looking for better words. The specific promise God gave David (through the preacher Nathan) forms one of the key parts of all Scripture: "I will make for you a name . . . a house . . . a place for my people . . . and your throne will be estab-

lished forever" (2 Sam. 7). But instead of trusting the promise, David immediately showed himself to be what Luther called "an enthusiast" (a "God-within-er" or a "navel theologian") who looked for better words than the ones he got. David, for example, was not content with God building him a house; he immediately wanted to seize the reins and build God a house. Isn't that good, religious fervor? What is wrong with David wanting to give something back to God? David launched off into creating his own words and worship of God, and by doing so David lost his ear for the shepherd's voice. God responded to him as if to say, "No, David, you have mixed up the subject and object—*I* will build *your* house." Luther observed that sin cannot be revealed in its depth and breadth until it is compared not only with the *law* but finally with God's word of *promise*.

The Messy Divorce

For Luther, David proved that learning about sin was not like learning the alphabet or learning about nature. You have heard people say God hates the sin and loves the sinner? Such people have never experienced God's wrath like David, where such fine distinctions just cannot be made. David found himself in direct and active opposition to God and under the immediate threat of death—with no escape. David's own righteousness before God "has been reduced to exactly nothing."[2] *Exactly nothing.* David finally saw that sin is not the compilation of misdeeds—things I actually did or left undone—but "in sin did my mother conceive me" (Ps. 51:5, au. trans.). He was having the depth of sin revealed to him—its "originality" and its inescapability.

What David needed in order to avoid the eternal despair of people like Pharaoh, was something to hang on to—a promise that would let him turn to the very God who was judging and condemning him. He needed God clothed in a word of promise so he could run from the naked God and its certain death. David was learning that sin affects God, not only "I, the sinner." God is no bean counter determining how many and what kind of sins have been committed and then, like a celestial accountant, doling out punishments and calmly determining who can make it through the pearly gates. Sin is like a messy divorce that is painful to watch and worse to go through. The sparring partners can never seem to separate far enough; the world grows narrow, and neither wife nor husband can stand even knowing the other walks the earth. Fights break out about the children, and jealousies grow into defensive posturing. The partners, who once were one body in joy become one body in misery—constantly fighting about who is right.

David felt this divorce as a "gigantic mountain of wrath," Luther noted, that had separated him from God. There and then he had to do one thing that is easy, and one that is incomparably hard. David called on the very God who was so angry with him that he didn't even want to see David's face or hear his voice because it was just too painful. But David called out anyway using God's proper name: "merciful." That was actually the easy part, at least for David (maybe not for God). The hard work, the mission impossible for a human will, is then to say to the angry God, "Have mercy on *me*." That little pronoun is always the problem. It declares to one's self and the world, "I am not right." It gives all the "right" to God and it asks that God do what is impossible for us in the middle of our messy divorce—just up and forgive for no reason but love.

Given this bitter feeling in the messy divorce with God, no wonder most people simply do not pray. True prayer

prays against itself, trusting that God is not done speaking once the law has been uttered. What does God do with bound and accused sinners like David—just up and forgive? Yes.

CHAPTER EIGHT

God, Who Forgives Sin:
The Gospel

For Luther, the second part of all theology is *God, who forgives sin*. Once Luther considered God as the one who justifies apart from the law by forgiving sinners, then Christ emerged from theological burial under years of defenses for free will and the church's own authority to bind sinners.

The Law, Until Christ

The law is not eternal! Who knew? When the apostle Paul got this message he was undone. Luther was scared, and then heaven opened. The law rules and lasts until Christ. At him, where he is (and only there), law ends. The question of what lies beyond good and evil has been asked from

Adam and Eve to the likes of Friedrich Nietzsche. For those who have built their theology on the one note of law, beyond good and evil there is nothing but chaos or supermen who make their own law—a tyrant or anarchy, take your poison. But for Luther a whole new world beyond good and evil showed itself in what the Bible calls "the gospel." What is this gospel? Luther answered, "The Gospel is a proclamation about Christ: that he forgives sins, grants grace, justifies and saves sinners. Although there are commandments in the New Testament, they are not the Gospel."[1] Gospel is not law; gospel is Jesus Christ given to you by a preacher as forgiveness in words and things.

The law had to be considered one way "before Christ" and another way "after (or under) Christ." This opened a series of controversial insights for Luther. First, the law "before Christ" had a history that developed over time in somewhat different ways for different cultures. Luther did not separate Old Testament law into a moral foundation that applied to everyone and a ceremonial law that applied only to Jews. He even called the Ten Commandments the Jewish form of his culture's *Sachsenspiegel* (Saxon code of law). As soon as Luther's students heard such things they naturally asked, "Why then preach about Moses if he has nothing to do with us?" Luther took up that very question in his striking sermon "How Christians Should Regard Moses." Luther gave three reasons to preach from the Old Testament: First, the Ten Commandments are "extraordinarily fine rules" that one would be wise to adopt for living because they agree with natural law and are a great mirror to hold up to your own culture and self. But the key is that you *may* select them for governing according to human reason. By 1525 Luther had become aware of what he called "false brethren," who wanted to reform the church by reinstituting the life of the Old Testament. The

Peasant Uprising in 1525 was encouraged by Thomas Müntzer, for example, by his taking God's words that belonged historically to the Jews and misapplying them to the German peasants.

Luther's second reason to preach from the Old Testament was that promises frequently are made therein that point to Christ, such as the blessing given to Abraham. His third reason was that he increasingly found the Old Testament loaded with examples of what it is like to have faith under "the cross" and to show acts of love that come from that trust. In that sense there is no great difference between a promise before or after Christ came. Job, Jeremiah, Abraham, Sarah, Hannah, and the like emerged as predecessors in faith who were given words from God to trust.

Luther was even bolder with the law "after Christ." The law did not disappear like smoke in thin air: "the law in all eternity will never be abolished but will remain either to be fulfilled in the damned or already fulfilled in the blessed."[2] Right there is the difference between being in heaven and being in hell—in hell the law remains forever ahead of you as something that needs yet to be done (like Sisyphus rolling his stone up and down without end); in heaven the law is past. In both cases the law has been completely historicized, and so you are always either ahead or behind it. For Luther, that spelled the end of the great theological attempt to describe life as the vision of God's great structure of being according to "laws"—an attempt that was nearly perfected by Thomas Aquinas's beatific vision.

Everything about your future hope depends upon Jesus Christ interrupting your life "before the law" and setting the law permanently behind you. How is that done?

It is not the superhuman self beyond good and evil, nor is it despair and chaos, but this particular man and Son of

God, Jesus Christ, alone stands resurrected beyond good and evil—the one who crawled from death to life to forgive you. Moses and the law cannot do that. Beyond your morality and works lies a new world of forgiveness where God forgets your sin because it lies on his Son, the lamb, and is nailed conclusively to his cross. How do you get beyond the hide-and-seek search for a better law and stronger will? Luther said to "turn away from good and evil; depend on Christ."[3] That means a preacher comes with the word of God's Son, who was made flesh, suffered, died, rose from the dead, and was glorified by the Spirit *for you*. The Holy Spirit's preacher throws out God's word like a farmer sowing seed, and this word communicates to a hearer everything that belongs to that word. Luther once put it this way: "If a touch of Christ healed, how much more will this most tender spiritual touch, this absorbing of the Word, communicate to the soul all things that belong to the Word."[4] At the heart of the gospel a double exchange takes place: Christ takes on the sinner's struggle with sin, Satan, and death; the sinner receives Christ's righteousness, life, and salvation. That exchange is how you are made "right" with God by faith without works of law. When a theologian investigates the gospel, most of the time must be spent on how Christ manages to accomplish this struggling and happy exchange when Moses and the law could not.

The Gospel in a Nutshell: "For You"

Aristotle used to say that when you define something you first say what it is not, then say what it is. So we have just said that gospel is not more law. What is it then? Who is this Jesus Christ, apart from whom we have no God, and what is his good news? Luther once gave "the gospel in a nutshell" in his provocative little book meant to help struggling consciences, *A Brief Instruction on What to Look for and Expect in the Gospels.* The gospel is just Jesus' story. "At its briefest," Jesus' story is this: "that he is the Son of God and became man for us, that he died and was raised, that he has been established as Lord over all things."[5] That is the gospel story in a nutshell.

But there is something else that must be said about Jesus' story. The gospel is not just a story *about* Jesus written in a book called "the Bible." The story needs a proper foundation that Luther called "the proper application of the pronoun" by which Jesus' story is preached and given "for *you*." "Before you do anything else with Christ, you take him as a gift,"[6] Luther insisted. Christ's story must function as law and gospel in your own life. That means that when Luther says "gospel" it includes not only Christ and what he did, but it also includes *you* as a sinner for whom he did it.

This gospel then requires that preachers be sent and hearers be made. But why is gospel so rare if the goal is to give Christ away, for free, as our righteousness? Don't people like free things? This is trickier than it might seem,

even though most people like the *idea* of a no-strings gift and would gladly accept any sweepstakes gift they "won" just for entering. The sticky matter lies in that part of the gospel that says, "He died." No one seems to want a dead Jesus on their hands, and so we have to enter into how it is that revulsion at the cross pushes Jesus back into the mold of a Moses where he can be immortalized in thought and we can spiritualize "communion" with him instead of having the real man Jesus burden us with his particular words and his accusing death. Sinners prefer an absent Jesus, and church leaders and theologians by Luther's day had actually perfected the arguments that made Christ absent so that they could "stand in" for him. So, Luther believed, it is in the church that you will necessarily find both Christ and anti-Christ at war.

The Word Became Flesh

Theology speaks *about* God (it has no "for you") and so is written. Proclamation speaks *for* God with its proper application of the pronoun in "for you"—and so is spoken. To preach rightly, Luther used the church's teaching about the incarnation (God in flesh) and multiplied it exponentially until people began to worry that Luther relished Christ's particularity and raw earthliness far too much. *Immanuel,* God with us, meant for Luther, "Christ is so much with us in the muck and work of our lives that his skin smokes."[7]

To teach preachers how to speak for Christ, Luther once took Paul's opening lines of the letter to the Galatians: "Grace to you and peace from God the Father and our Lord Jesus Christ," and asked, Why did Paul add to an already good Hebrew blessing the words "and our Lord Jesus Christ"? Answer: Because Christian faith "does not begin at the top, as all other religions do; it begins at the bottom."[8] Where is "the bottom"? Theologies have always divided on the matter of where to start speaking about God. Some start with the Son of God, the second person of the Trinity and God's Word who, as the evangelist John wrote, is God before all creation and through whom all things were made. Then suggestions follow concerning how it was possible that this eternal, infinite God became incarnate in one person. For such top-down theologians the "fit" of the incarnation is something of a problem. A very big God seems to have a hard time fitting into the skin of a very small Mediterranean peasant, and somehow the truth of the human Jesus gets overwhelmed by absorption. Such theologians are not good at the incarnation or the death of Christ on the cross. In fact, such theologians tend to be prudish and protective of God's divinity, making sure no one disgraces God with two many bodily functions or with human despair—and certainly not dying! So theories developed about how Jesus Christ was God playing a dramatic role as a man (Docetism). Christian gnostics liked to tell made-up stories about how Jesus did spectacular things

as an infant and growing boy, but somehow he never seemed quite "normal."

On the other hand, one could find theologians who started with the man Jesus according to their understanding of what makes a real human. Didn't Jesus cry? Didn't he feel desires for a woman like a man would feel (read *The Last Temptation of Christ*)? But then for such theologians how do you begin talking about Christ as "divine" and able to save? Maybe there were two sons, or two souls? Maybe he was open to higher powers, or was a very "spiritual" child who had a kind of sixth sense? Theirs was a problem of size in reverse: How big, powerful, and eternal can you make Jesus without losing humanity? Divinity for them became an abstract idea or category that sounded fuzzy, like "community," or "justice," or "openness to the future." Maybe God adopted the man Jesus? Maybe Jesus got elevated to divinity on the basis of good behavior? Maybe we live in the communal effects of Jesus' love like ripples in a pool of water set off by his tiny pebble? These sorts of theologians are never very good at the Trinity or resurrection, since they prefer to concentrate on "real" things they can confirm or deny by history or science or by staring at their own navel. In fact, they are liable to be on the idealist or romantic side, starting off sounding earthy about all that Jesus experienced or stood for in his life, then they go "spiritual" with obscure suggestions about how Jesus and his example can lift us into a greater sense of love and community as in the "Fatherhood of God and the brotherhood of man" that nineteenth-century liberal Christianity affirmed.

Between these two groups is another, associated with a third-century priest named Arius, who suggested a compromise between top-down and bottom-up theology: How about starting in between? Jesus is neither man nor God but a "third thing." Arius sang monotone according to the law, and so believed in a Monad (one) before there was a Dyad (two). Maybe, he thought, the incarnation was God dipping his toe into flesh to see what it is like, then returning to his throne where he really belongs and waiting for humans to catch his spirit? By the fourth century, Christians found themselves in a fix, since Arian churches held the day—especially among the bishops and emperors. But Arians haven't got much to preach, since God cannot quite get down to us as sinners and we cannot quite get up to God who is perfect, so the whole church hung suspended between heaven and earth like Absalom hanging by his hair, as Luther liked to say.

Luther took such christological debates away from talking *about* Jesus Christ and identified what happened when one began speaking *for* Jesus Christ. He took Christology out of speculation and put it into proclamation. In other words, Luther began thinking like a preacher whose job is hope, instead of a philosopher whose job is ontology (what *is*).

When Luther said to "begin below," he did not mean to start with your picture of the historical Jesus and work your way higher. He meant something specific and quite disturbing (or comforting, depending on your way of hearing it). Begin with your God, your ultimate judge who holds the power of the law, *sucking his mother's milk* at the breast. Begin with your God in the womb, so that the jarring fear of having to account to God for your life may subside long enough to hear what God promised. Luther believed the church was exactly right to reject Arianism as its worst heresy at the council of Nicaea (A.D. 325), and was at least beginning to give its positive description of the gospel at the council of Chalcedon (A.D. 451) in the form of the doctrine of Christ's "communication of attributes" (*communicatio idiomatum*), which held that Jesus Christ is truly divine and truly human "in two natures, unconfusedly, immutably, indivisibly, indistinctly."[9] Yet the church's teaching needed to be more radical in order to get out of the way of Christ's arrival.

The only end to the game of hide-and-seek is finding the omnipotent God in the lowly manger of Christ's birth, for there you find your *gracious* God. Today we often hear people say they really want to believe in something, to get religion, or that they are launching spiritual quests. But

Luther believed that all quests end not on a mountaintop, nor in mystical contemplation, nor in great works of justice, but at Christ in the manger and hearing that this is God *for us* while we were yet sinners.

Nestorius, an Altogether Mad "Saint"

The church has long been ambivalent or hostile to its own central teaching. Even when it has rejected a false teaching it has had difficulty being positive about how to give Jesus Christ to sinners without conditions. In particular it has usually balked at two key moments in its announcement to the world: "God died for you," and "We have no other God than this man, Jesus." At the very moment preachers are to hand over these words as law and gospel to ungodly people, they become tongue-tied and pull back from the brink of what seems irrational mercy on the part of God. God so incarnate seems to ask too much of God or give too much to undeserving humans.

The "lofty articles of divine Majesty" (Trinity and incarnation) were drawn by Luther from the "chief" article of justification by faith alone. The God who forgives is Father, Son, and Holy Spirit; Christ the Son is the one who became a man and "was handed over to death for our trespasses and was raised for our justification" (Rom. 4:25 au. trans.). "On this article (justification) stands all that we teach and practice against the pope, the devil, and the world." So Luther continued, "Therefore we must be quite certain and have no doubt about it. Otherwise everything is lost."[10] This clarity gave Luther unparalleled audacity in getting preachers to do their jobs. To see how Luther went beyond the Council of Chalcedon, we can consider Luther's own assessment of the Nestorian controversy of the fifth century in *On the Councils and the Church*.

Nestorius was bishop of Constantinople after 428, when a court chaplain refused to allow the word *Theotokos* in worship. *Theotokos* was by then a reference to Mary as the "bearer of God." Nestorius agreed to ban such liturgical language because "strictly speaking" Mary could only be mother to a human and at most you could say in prayers, hymns, or sermons that she gave birth to Christ but not to God. But then the question followed: What was the evangelist John saying by "the Word became flesh"? Nestorius preferred to say that God was "conjoined" to humans, but as Lutherans were to say later, this meant the human and divine in Jesus were like two boards glued together with no "communion" or interpenetration.

Nestorius, Luther concluded, was "an altogether mad saint and ignorant man" because he would not admit a *communicatio idiomatum* for fear of mixing human and divine into some other substance. Yet, as the ancient theologian and opponent of Nestorius, Cyril of Alexandria, once argued that if Mary is not "strictly speaking" the

Mother of God, and Jesus is her Son, then Jesus would not "strictly speaking" be God. The big controversy in Luther's own day was the specific words of the Lord's Supper: Jesus said, "Take and eat, for this is my body, given for you." How could Jesus be giving his body in the bread? Luther recognized that this question (put to him by Zwingli, then Oecolampadius, then Bucer, and finally his own friend Melanchthon) was the same sort that had bothered Nestorius about Mary bearing God. People always prefer a pure idea of God to the dirty presence of Jesus, to God in your muck with smoking skin.

The Council of Chalcedon laid the pattern for preachers: "Say of Christ that he is one person, with two natures." Unfortunately, this allowed cowards to equivocate when it came to preaching. If Jesus Christ did something unusual, such as calm the sea or forgive sins, it was attributed to his "divine nature." If something happened to Christ, such as

weeping or despairing or suffering or dying, it was attributed to his "human nature." So if a smart confirmation student asked how Jesus could have withstood Satan's temptation in the wilderness, the answer was, "His divine nature." If the same smart student asked how Christ could die on the cross, even though he was God, the answer was, "His human nature died." But Luther noted that not only do those answers fail to solve such questions, but they also take away the very heart of the gospel. This system misuses the "two natures" doctrine by failing to plunge into the *communicatio idiomatum*.

An *idioma* is a thing, or an attribute, that we use to speak of what it means to be a human—for example, dying, suffering, weeping, speaking, laughing, eating, drinking, sleeping, being born, having a mother, suckling the breast. If we switch to "things" that apply to God's nature, the list would be quite different: immortal, omnipotent, infinite, not born, does not eat or sleep, and so forth. Nestorius wanted to hold God and humans far apart so that God could *stay* holy and humans could be *made* holy and perfect. Once assured of the distinction he gladly would talk, no doubt, about humans becoming like God. Theologians such as Nestorius (or his opposite, Eutyches) will allow one side of the incarnation but not both. In Nestorius's case a human being lifted up (but never fully reaching divinity) was fine, but he was troubled by God *coming down*.

Luther then made his crucial contribution. Nestorius might be fine as a philosophy teacher (although syllogisms have to work both ways), but he doesn't know a thing about preaching Christ. If a preacher says to the congregation of sinners, "*Jesus* the carpenter of Nazareth is walking down the street to fetch water," Nestorius would say "fine." But then if the preacher says, "There goes *God* down the street fetching water," Nestorius would get all flustered because this wasn't the sort of thing God did—more to the point, it wouldn't leave any water for *humans* to fetch. That is why Luther called Nestorius proud and stubbornly stupid. He did not want God sullied by bodily things, and he wanted to save room for humans to do the works of the law. He did not want to preach that "God died," nor did he want to preach that "this man Jesus created the world."

Why not? He did not want God unholy and tied to what he took the problem of humans to be—their bodies—and so he did not want God demeaned, abased, humiliated, and degraded by not only *having* a body but *being* one. He did not want a particular person to be God, but preferred the old "fuzzy" theology of the incarnation by which "humanity" as a general category is somehow made divine. Luther smelled the same old dead rat underneath Nestorius's rigid prudishness. The human free will must be protected, even against God's intrusion, so that it can cooperate or aid in the process of rising above the body to become more holy as we move toward the goal of perfection. His issue wasn't really Mary after all; it was the attempt to protect God from disgrace and to leave room for a noble free will.

The basic problem, Luther concluded, was that Nestorius held the right doctrine of the two natures and the one person (if he had gotten that question on a test he would have passed), but he refused the *communicatio idiomatum*, which is the way of announcing that God has really come *to you* while you were yet a sinner, to interrupt you permanently on your path to righteousness by the law. Moreover, God did this by becoming this particular man, Jesus Christ, who was born of Mary, under the law (Gal. 4:4), and was crucified and died. He is also the same person who was raised and has a kingdom of new creatures given to him by the Holy Spirit. The one reason for the Chalcedonian doctrine in the first place was to lead to actual preaching in which Christ comes to sinners in the "for you" of actual forgiveness. Statements such as "She bore God" or "God died" find their proper place in preaching, prayer, and hymns. Nestorius had the right *doctrine*, but not the right *proclamation*. As an abstract idea, "Mary bore God" is false. As an address to a sinner "for you," it functions as the *law* for those who take offense at such a God and his love, and the *gospel* for those who in faith receive it as God's deep, loving, and intractable act for them while they were yet sinners. What teaching or ideas *cannot* do, proclamation *must* do. Church doctrine can speak of Jesus Christ in two natures and one person, but it cannot say by itself, "Here he is, for you."

A Big, Fat God

Luther's Christology comes out in his upside-down use of an old illustration in *On the Councils and Churches*. If justice is like a woman blindfolded and holding scales with two pans, then you and your sin weigh more than you can ever repay. How can you ever get your pan to balance with God's? That much was a common description of sin, such as you would find in Anselm. But then Luther reversed the image. What sinners need is a big, fat God who takes up room in the world and can outweigh our Faustian selves grown enormous on self-righteous lusts. Sinners do not need a skinny, monastic God who somehow slips into and out of a body; they need an incarnate tub of lard to come down so hard and deep into the world that when God sits in the other pan of the scales we bounce up like we were on the slight end of a teeter-totter. Luther is even willing to pause for a minute and talk about Christ's body being

wherever Christ is—and that means everywhere present! Of course, this makes human reason and its buff, free will feel crowded out of the world. This teaching of Christ as a fat, immovable presence in the world became a big argument following Luther's death. Both students and friends of Luther, as well as later reformers such as John Calvin, asked incredulously, What kind of a fat monster would Christ be if his body were wherever his divinity was?

It gets worse, since Luther also was perfectly willing to talk about the fullness of God being wherever the particular man Jesus is. Luther completely reversed normal descriptions of "assumption" found in so-called Logos Christologies, where an incarnate God somehow subsumes humanity and makes it more perfectly "divine." Luther's assumption theory is not preoccupied with how humans get up into the divine but how the divine goes so deep into our flesh that he gives his weight to sinful human flesh (our desire to escape into "spiritual" matters that we think are "higher" than body). When God sits his corpulent mercy down in this world, no spiritual diet or holy crane will ever get him out again. Sinners "go up" to being real human beings for the first time because he "came down" like an enormous divine weight that won't move. Consequently for Luther, salvation is not taking leave of humanity and becoming like God; it is becoming really and fully human as God's own trusting creature in Christ's new kingdom. Being human means receiving everything in creation from God through trusting his promises day by day.

The *communicatio idiomatum* meant for Luther that we have no other God than this particular man Jesus. We are

stuck with him, even though he does not appeal to our religious fantasies of a God who somehow includes all of the people and religions of the earth in some grand theory that finally makes sense to our generous reason. Further, in Jesus Christ, divine and human are not like two boards glued together, nor are they a mixture of a new kind, but they have so penetrated each other that we can no longer know what God is like without starting with Jesus. Likewise the reverse: We don't really know what a human is without starting with Jesus. Everything God is, is right there in him—creator, eternal, unthwartable in his will, predestinating, merciful. And this God is so deep in the flesh that when he comes to sit down on earth he is not going anywhere else and refuses to be moved out of the way by spiritual hide-and-seekers. You can almost hear him say, "Over my dead body."

CHAPTER NINE

At Great Cost: How Christ's Cross Saves Sinners

The righteous one, my servant, shall make many righteous, and he shall bear their iniquities.

(Isaiah 53:11)

If we could be made right by any other means, then what in the world is Christ doing on the cross? Over and over Luther confronted sinners with this relentless reckoning. If Christ died for us while we were his enemies (and the cross confirms that), then how much more will his resurrected life save us? (Rom. 5:10).

What Happened When Jesus Christ Came Near?

Since Luther insisted that we start with our God in the manger, he is also insistent that we not misrepresent the story of what actually happened to Christ when he came to dwell among his own creatures. Jesus came into the world not as a king, at least not recognizably, or a magician, or a revolutionary, but as a *preacher*. But preaching was where the trouble with Jesus started, since he proceeded to act like he could out-and-out forgive sins just like God. To the paralytic, Jesus said, "Son, your sins are forgiven," and murmuring arose: "It is blasphemy! Who can forgive sins but God alone?" (Mark 2:5–7).

The whole story of Jesus finally concerns whether he can forgive sins or not, despite all human objections to the practice. As Luther said in one of his most famous lines from the *Small Catechism,* "Where there is forgiveness of sins there is also life and salvation." What happened to Jesus when he just peremptorily forgave sins as one who has authority? It got him killed.

So far that is enough for Jesus' story: He was a man who forgave sins like God and got killed for it. Now what possible good could come from such a crime? An imaginary free will that cooperates with grace for its own salvation always wants more time. For what? For giving God what he wants, for getting better words, or for playing hide-and-seek to buy time and space for its own hopes. A dead Jesus throws a monkey wrench into this plan, as Luther saw, and consequently the teaching of Christ's two natures has been repeatedly used to deny that when *Jesus* died, *God* also died. After all, if God died, who would uphold the legal structure of the world so your will has *time* to become righteous?

That is why Christ was given no space in this old world

where people try to become righteous by the law: "Foxes have holes, and birds of the air have nests; but the Son of Man has nowhere to lay his head" (Matt. 8:20). He was judged by the ruling authorities as one whose "time was up." Humans have no time or place on earth for God and his forgiveness, since that very mercy permanently disrupts order and ends the charade of original sin that looks for better words than Jesus' forgiveness of sin. So Jesus was crucified by religious, political, and moral people attempting to hold to the old time and its law—that is, to protect human space and time against God's premature and permanent interruption.

For our own self-preservation God was humiliated, raised on the criminal's cross, placed outside the gate (Heb. 13:12), outside the temple in the place where animal dung

and discarded intestines were burned in order to keep the place of sacrifice to God holy. Jesus was treated like the worst opponent of what is right in the world, and like so much trash was discarded so the world could go on with its manufactured quest for holiness. The Creator of the world (Logos) entered the world, and the world knew him not (John 1:10). How odd! He became a curse for us, under the very holy law, which we used to condemn him. He became sin (Gal. 3:13). He was despised and had no one to comfort him (Isa. 53). Yet, even if you are somehow touched by this pathos, you might rightly ask, What good does it do to keep going over it? What good is all of that "for you" now?

Christ the Curse

The church has had a series of theories about how Christ dying on the cross could possibly be good for you and the world. It often calls them "atonement" theories, and by Luther's time there were basically three. One understood the cross as the final defeat of Satan in a cosmic battle, but the victory came by means of a deceit—God deceived Satan into taking his Son and giving up rights to the world's sinners. That came perilously close to the Manichean belief in two gods fighting to the death; more-over, it made God himself lawless by stooping to trick the devil. Anselm's later alternative deepened the church's emphasis on Christ's cross as a substitute sacrifice that paid the debt sinners owed to an angry and just God. God decided to count Christ's death as payment for all previous debt. Yet that arrangement seemed curiously to take place without the sinners themselves and under the cover of divine, slight-of-hand bookkeeping. A third theory, reacting against Anselm, emphasized Christ as the one who shows us the way to lay down our lives for others out of love. But not only is that imitation of Christ's love notoriously hard to do, it also seemed to make Christ's death itself only an example and not redemption once and for all. Luther used touches of all these theories, since they each have certain biblical roots, but he saw in all of them a basic problem. They all turned on the refusal to announce that Jesus actually became a sinner, the greatest of all sinners—even sin itself. Luther emphatically changed that.

In 1534 Luther lectured to his students on Galatians for a second time. In speaking about the climax of the letter, Luther dwelt on two closely related phrases from the apostle Paul: "For our sake he made him to be sin who knew no sin" (2 Cor. 5:21) and "Christ redeemed us from the curse of the law by becoming a curse for us" (Gal. 3:13). Both of those verses were drawn from the single most important sentence of the Bible for Luther: "All we like sheep have gone astray; we have all turned to our own way, and the LORD has laid on him the iniquity of us all" (Isa. 53:6).

Luther started his theology of the cross as Paul did: Jesus knew no sin, but *for our sake* God made him to *be sin*. Luther then saw the problem in the subsequent Bible commentaries. They agreed that Jesus knew no sin, but balked at the bald assertion that Jesus *became sin* for us. Yet if you take that out then you remove forgiveness itself. Then heaven is dependent on your finding ways to get rid of the sin you still bear (like the church's system of penance). Luther referred to Jerome, but we can conveniently use Anselm's famous treatise *Why God Became Man* to see the inner problem:

> Therefore man cannot and ought not by any means
> to receive from God what God designed to give him,

151

unless he return to God everything which he took from him; so that, as by man God suffered loss, by man, also, He might recover His loss. But this cannot be effected except in this way: that, as in the fall of man all human nature was corrupted, and, as it were, tainted with sin, and God will not choose one of such a race to fill up the number in his heavenly kingdom; so, by man's victory, as many men may be justified from sin as are needed to complete the number which man was made to fill. *But a sinful man can by no means do this, for a sinner cannot justify a sinner.*[1]

Luther arrayed his full army of arguments against this embedded rejection of Jesus Christ's cross as having "finished" the matter of sin. You say a sinner cannot justify a sinner? Well, Luther said, Jesus is not only a sinner, but he became "a curse for us." On top of that he "has sinned or has sins." Moreover, Jesus was "sinner of sinners" and "the highest, the greatest, and the *only* sinner."[2] And in near madness (were forgiveness itself not at stake) Christ became sin itself.

If your trust lies elsewhere, such as in logic's fundamental principle of ontology (that a thing cannot have one attribute and its opposite at the same time), then Christ who is sinless and sinful at the same time must be rejected. What is much more important, a false doctrine of justification aimed at protecting one's own righteousness repeatedly refuses to hear Paul's sermon to the Galatians at this point. Anselm and the Christian theologians demanded *purity* from their redeemer and defended him from the ignominy of the curse of the law: "A sinner cannot save a sinner." Thus, in one fell swoop, theologians tried to protect Christ, the law, and themselves from unrighteousness, and thereby ended up calling God a liar. They searched for better words than "Christ became a curse."

Luther understood that as long as your feet are planted in the law as the way to be right, you can never bear the cross or its unadulterated forgiveness of sins: "In short, our sin must be *Christ's own sin,* or we shall perish eternally."[3] If Christ's sin is a fiction, then so is our salvation. Why, Luther asked, do people want to deny that Christ became a curse? He chose the very best of theologians, Thomas Aquinas, to demonstrate the problem. Aquinas argued that faith alone cannot save but instead faith must be "formed by love" or have acts of love added to it as directed by the law. Luther saw the problem. Theologians who refuse Christ as a curse want their sin removed not *in Christ* but *in themselves.* They can only think of sin ontologically, as something that really sticks to them as color sticks to a wall. Then, they think, getting rid of that sin must be the reversal of what got it there in the first place; lack of charity can only be overcome by getting charity back inside the heart and will. You can't just trust Christ outside your own self to be your very own righteousness before Almighty God; you have to manufacture righteousness in yourself. Luther called that an old, pious wish—to be valuable in one's self and right in relation to the law—even by grace upon grace being poured in. People want to be biographically or narratively righteous in their own selves. Luther thought that not only were such people singing monotone but their one single note was of course always the same. It was the song of the self, expressing its innards to the world as if that were salvation and upon hearing it the world would fall down and worship at their feet. The secret underlying this rejection of Christ as the greatest of all sinners was a driving desire not to be blamed for Christ's death and especially to avoid having Christ's cross applied to oneself. In short, people do not want to die under God's wrath.

This rather simple and "innocent" desire to be righteous in oneself and not in Christ alone (and so to avoid death) became the basic confusion of law and gospel that ended in a terrible double bind: Such people "segregate Christ from sins and from sinners."[4] Christians constantly fall into this mess theologically by making up their own words so that Christ (who is holy and clean) will make us holy and clean according to the old pagan rule: "Like likes like." Socrates, Plato, Aristotle, and all the philosophers argued this way. If you want to become a horse trainer, to whom do you go? To someone who is already skilled at training horses. If you want to be righteous, to whom do you go? To one who is already skilled at being righteous. Who wants to go to a loser God? To a dead Jesus? Who wants to go to a *sinner* who died under the curse of the cross? People do not want their righteousness to be in Christ alone; they want to be molded into the right image in themselves so that justification *starts* with faith but *ends* with a life full of acts of love that imitates Christ's perfect life. But for Luther, sinners are on a hide-and-seek mission to become righteous in themselves by using Christ *temporarily* like a puff of oxygen from a tank, but never would they willingly allow themselves to be on life-support forever. After all, wouldn't that make you a vegetable instead of an authentic human who is trying her best to be pure? Wouldn't you rather be dead than on life-support forever?

Christians like Anselm have argued that my *penalty* may have lain on Christ but not my *sins*, since Christ must be sinless that I might aspire to become like him. If he is sin, the whole system crashes. Law would come to an end. Your justification would be in Christ only, not in yourself. No matter how hard you try, you just cannot make Jesus' death on the cross a goal that you are trying to reach. You would then feel death and God's wrath at your sin and die with a despairing confession on your lips: "My God, my God, why have your forsaken me?" (Mark 15:34).

So here you come to a crossroads, Luther thought. You have to learn to make "the right division," not according to the logic of the law but the logic of the cross's law and gospel. If Christ "is innocent and does not carry our sins, then we carry them and shall die and be damned in them." That is Paul's "irrefutable antithesis."[5] Either the sin belongs to Christ and is defeated in him alone, or it belongs to me and there remains eternally while I remain under God's wrath. Luther urged his students to quit defending Christ's honor from sin in order to keep their own honor before God's law. Learn to apply law and gospel, justification by faith alone, to Christ and his cross, and you begin to see a frightening and freeing thing. The predicate "sin" really belongs to the subject "Christ" in such a way that there your sin ends. *Christ became sin for you.*

Learning How to Lay Your Sins on Jesus, the Lamb

When humans have set up their false righteousness according to the law and their imaginary free will, the only means left for God to interrupt their wild search is to lose by the very rules of their own game of hide-and-seek. This is why Luther is so careful to draw out Paul's insistence that Christ's death was a curse *according to the law*. Jesus' death was not a case of mistaken identity. Neither was it a bump on the road to greater discipleship for those following him. More specifically, the law was not misused by the Sanhedrin in a miscarriage of justice. Nor were the Romans naively trying to keep the lid on a revolutionary situation.

156

The law was used against Christ in its most holy and high form of justice at the height of its power (just as death, devil, curse, wrath, and sin were also in play at the height of their powers). The legal mode of thinking was taken on at its best and defeated—by losing.

This is the great secret of the battle between curse and blessing on the cross, between law and gospel. God shows you where the game of hide-and-seek inevitably ends, then God does a new thing by forgiving deicidal maniacs with a promise that does exactly what it says: "Blessed are those whose iniquities are forgiven, and whose sins are covered. . . . It will be reckoned to us who believe in him who raised Jesus our Lord from the dead, who was handed over to death for our trespasses and was raised for our justification" (Rom. 4:7, 24–25). Your search for better words than Christ is doomed, but Christ's word raises the dead into a new life beyond the law.

This finally led Luther to what he called "the great and *delicious* language" for preaching, or the "Hebraic idiom." Luther understood that the main work of a theologian is

translation. He explained in two important essays, "On Translating" and "Defense of Translating the Psalms," why he had to add the famous word "alone" to the German translation of Romans 3:28: "For we hold that one is justified by faith *alone* apart from works of law." Why? Because Paul's whole purpose is to cut away all good works of law from what makes one justified. In that case a faithful translator must add a *particula exclusiva,* an exclusive word, to make Paul's argument clear. The opposite case also happens. At times a translator must stay with the literal words of a text, even if they sound awkward in the new language. Luther's favorite example of that came from his translation of Psalm 68:18: "thou hast led captivity captive" (au. trans.). It is bad German, he admitted, to undo a noun with its verbal form, but he kept the awkward phrase on account of the true "doctrine" therein. He made "room for the Hebrew" where German was inadequate. Nothing conveys better what the communication of attributes means for sinners than this Hebrew version of the exchange: Christ has become the *death of your death,* as Hosea sings, "O death, I shall be your death!" (Hos. 13:14, au. trans.).

How does God get rid of sin? By sinning against sin. How does God get rid of killing? By killing killing. How does God end your game of hide-and-seek? By losing a losing game. How does the law come to an end? By judging the law! But before this can really be delicious language it must be seen as highly precarious. Because the curse is God's own wrath at sin, and because Christ is God himself, when Christ's cross is preached you become a party to a struggle between God and God—in Christ: "Therefore the curse clashes with the blessing and wants to damn it and annihilate it. But it cannot. For the blessing is divine and eternal, and therefore the curse must yield to it. For if the blessing in Christ could be conquered, then God Himself would be conquered. . . . But this is impossible," Luther concluded in his Galatians lectures.[6]

God's "alien" will in the cross has been conquered by his "proper" will "for you." God won by losing your game and starting up his own game of forgiving sinners by raising them from the dead—no hide-and-seek being desired or necessary. Once you are raised from the dead by Christ's promise, death can no longer be feared. It lies behind you instead of threatening your future at every turn. The law and its demand becomes a past event, not a present threat or future goal. "Who shall bring any charge against God's elect?" Paul asked. If Christ is the final judge and he killed killing by being raised from the dead and forgiving his sinners, then what further judgment do you fear? The sting of death is removed because Christ unilaterally forgave and so interrupted your life permanently. Laying your sins on Jesus means they are over and have no more power to slip into your conscience to say, "What have you done?" Instead, Christ alone sits there calling his sheep by name and freely giving them all they need. Paul confessed that in such a new circumstance nothing (not death, sin, or devil) can "separate us from the love of God in Christ Jesus our Lord" (Rom. 8:38–39).

In Christ, God's curse attacks God's blessing, and when the Father raises his only begotten Son from the grave we have a new time, a new kingdom, a new creation, whose "firstfruits" are Christ himself—body and all resurrected from the dead (1 Cor. 15). The Holy Spirit glorifies Christ as the Lord of the new creation, giving him everything that is raised from the dead and so lives eternally.

Though we did not want God's forgiveness lest we die, and so we did not give Christ time or place on earth, God stages a great reversal. To our eternal surprise, God has created a new time and place; the Father raised Christ, the loser, from the dead. Now this Christ has time for us—even while we were yet ungodly and looking about for better words. He has room for us and we are present to him in the new, unprecedented time and place made by the Holy Spirit. Though this is hidden from sight, it is available for faith and so is rightly a present, spiritual kingdom.

In light of this great reversal, Luther taught preachers a new language. Christ has come for you in masks—both from above and below, larger than large, smaller than small—as the power of the Lord to forgive through created things: Christ's body and blood, water, bread and wine, and the frail words of the sinful preacher. Not only does Christ run faster than sinners who are running from his word, but he is able to come at them from both directions at once! No escape! Mercy is in this way unthwartable, irresistible, foreknown, predestined, and you are passively formed, called, justified, and glorified (Rom. 8:28). So when the preacher comes you just have to bear the awful truth that your sins are forgiven on account of Christ *alone*.

CHAPTER TEN

This Is My Body:
God's Means of Grace

Take; eat; this is my body which is given for you.
(Matthew, Mark, Luke, and Paul)

Where is Christ the gracious God found deep in the flesh so as to help dying sinners? Christ's death saves only when it is preached for you; otherwise, it sits in history as implacable judgment. Luther thought that when the cross was really preached the communication of attributes in Christ's own person would extend out telescopically as an *exchange* between Christ and sinners that would be both awful and joyous. What Christ won by losing is a new kingdom of true Spirit where sins are forgiven apart from the law in Christ himself, souls are cured, and displaced consciences find their home. Everything sinners are and have Christ takes (the awful), and everything Christ is and has he gives to sinners (the joyous). If you are a sinner, what Christ gives is the deal of a lifetime. If you are holy, you must fight against this to your dying breath.

How is the exchange made? How will you ever stop your addiction to the possibility of better words? How does Christ break through the game of hide-and-seek? By giving words that may not be ignored, idealized, and otherwise turned into one's own act of righteousness, that is, external words that are "clingable." To people searching beyond God's created world and given words he gives "things," or masks of creation, you can hang onto with all five senses, and thereby hang on to God himself in trust. As Luther once put it in his *Smalcald Articles*, "God is extravagantly rich in his grace." He continued by saying that God gives help against this sin of hide-and-seek "in more than one way. . . . [F]irst, through the spoken word, in which the forgiveness of sins is preached to the whole world (which is the proper function of the gospel); second, through baptism; third, through the holy Sacrament of the Altar; fourth, through the power of the keys and also through the mutual conversation and consolation of brothers and sisters, Matthew 18[:20]: 'Where two or three are gathered. . . .'"[1] Sometimes those who followed Luther's cause abbreviated even this by saying that faith comes by "Word and sacrament" and that these alone make the new kingdom of Christ, the church.

The Preached Word Is Sacramental

God wants true worship, but inveterate hide-and-seekers are always trying to adore God outside his words planted in the world. To worship God rightly requires much more than good intentions or a great religious tradition. God's own words promising forgiveness are needed. Over and over again Luther dealt with the problem of "spiritualizing" the Word and sacraments by self-appointed preachers who tried to improve worship of God with their *own* version of the spoken word, baptism, the Lord's Supper, absolution, and "the mutual conversation and consolation of brothers and sisters."

The most important of God's ways of forgiving sins was by means of a preacher announcing law and gospel from the words of Scripture "for you." Such preaching was the way God gave the "precious keys" for heaven itself, which were first received in baptism, to all believers. In baptism Christ's promise of forgiveness was attached to water, and by being given to original sinners it imparted to them the power of the keys to forgive and condemn. Luther then referred to such forgiven sinners as "the priesthood of all believers," a holy priesthood (1 Pet. 2:5) that was not reserved for a special class of people sacramentally ordained. There were actually two keys given; one to lock the prison door of human sin and the other to open the door of heaven by the forgiveness of sins. Your prison door always opens from the outside, since the will is bound up with itself and requires someone to put a key in the lock and turn it. Turning the key is done by an external preacher actually declaring, "I forgive your sins on account of Christ." For that reason, when Luther was asked to help the church in Leisnig get a decent public worship he first asked the town church to restore the office of preaching so

163

that they "never gather together without preaching of God's Word and prayer, no matter how briefly."[2] Much of Luther's cause came down to this matter of getting priests to quit being "Mass priests" and to become preachers of the word. After all, there were dying souls in desperate need of faith, Luther thought. There was no time to spare! No office could ever get higher in Christ's kingdom or have more authority than preacher—not even bishop. Opening heaven's door for an imprisoned sinner is the most important act of life and cannot be superceded or controlled for distribution by a pope. For Luther, the authority of baptized people to free other sinners never submits to a higher law because such royal priests are living beyond that law.

Another question kept arising in Luther's day: Can anyone who "feels the spirit" preach at any time or place? An abundance of self-appointed prophets were putting themselves forward as God's spiritual messengers all over Germany by the 1520s. Luther called them "spiritualists," among less printable things.

Spiritualists ran about the country convincing people they were full of holiness by showing some sign or another of "spiritual" power. Luther recognized that the easiest attack on a *true* preacher was the same that Christ received: By what authority do you forgive sins? When the question comes, and it always does, preachers cannot rely on their own inner experience of a sense of "call" but must rely on the fact that they did not call or appoint themselves. An external call was essential for this purpose so that a preacher would not depend upon an inner feeling that is as fleeting as the wind. Ordination, however, as the church's traditional way of recognizing a call to the priesthood (a call that was already given) was not a sacrament itself that gave special powers to preachers. The authority of preachers remained always with the word of God alone to do just what was promised—forgive sinners.

But who can give the external call to the preacher? Once, the power to call and send preachers was Christ's alone when he called out disciples. But Luther believed Christ passed this authority to his preachers, whose words assemble the church of sinners, and so Luther noted the call can come either by the successors to the apostles, called bishops (Titus 1:5), or "by a prince or a magistrate or me."[3] Always the local church seeking a public preacher was included in the matter of who would be given the responsibility of serving them. By giving such a fluid list of who could call a preacher, Luther was not making new canon (or church) law, but was providing an illustration of how a public, external call could come. He could include himself in the list of callers because he was called to be a teacher of the whole church, as all would acknowledge. Many times when Luther's great temptation was put before him—"Are you the only one who knows?"—Luther responded with the certainty of his *external* call: "I am a doctor of the church, and so am bound to the word of Scripture," regardless of how few or many have believed. But it was always the content of the preaching of Christ crucified with its effect on sinners as law and gospel (the two absolutes) that alone really kill and make alive. No human traditions about who was allowed to call pastors to public service could displace that proclamation (as if they gave their own authority to help people believe the gospel). But neither could people decide to call themselves out of the crowd because they "felt the spirit."

Luther was careful about the office of preaching and who fills it because he believed preaching was God's own unthwartable desire to choose or elect sinners for Christ's new kingdom. So we return to the old question: What if

God doesn't send a preacher to me? Well, Luther would say, it is time to take the bull by the horns and get one yourself. Have you no free will in things beneath you? Can't you amble wherever you want, whenever you want? Of course, when you get there, to an assembly or church that has been made by a preacher's words, it will not be your free will that is in charge but a new power and freedom of God's that will take matters from there.

What if someone at some remote place does not get a preacher—isn't it God's fault then? In the abstract it would be God's fault, but this very question would implicate the one asking it. Having heard God's word, and knowing of others who have not heard, it is no longer possible to sit thinking up hypothetical reasons not to believe or why God should not be God. Once given a sure promise that establishes a hope in something beside your hypothetical free will, the only reasonable thing to do is serve whatever persons cross your path that have not heard by proclaiming the gospel to them.

The Nestorian Hangover in the Church: The Pope's Canon and Zwingli's *Alleosis*

In a remarkable effort that Luther thought would be his last, he wrote a final will and testament in 1527 centered on the words given at Christ's Supper: "This is my body, given for you." Luther's testament served not only to refute the Swiss reformer Zwingli, but it also became the basis for what would be the public confession of evangelicals, namely, the Augsburg Confession of 1530, which has been shared by many to the present day (who are usually called *Lutherans*). Luther's "Confession concerning Christ's Supper" would also become one of the centerpieces for later controversies among Lutherans and Calvinists in the generation following Luther. At the heart of the confession was Luther's belief that "apart from this man [i.e., Jesus Christ] there is no God."[4] He believed both the sacramentarians (and their offshoots "the false brethren" or spiritualists) and the papal party buried faith in Christ under one form or another of the search for purity according to the law.

Before he even knew anything about Nestorius, Luther said, he had to fight Zwingli and the sacramentarians on the basis of Scripture alone. But then Luther came to the conclusion that Zwingli's problem of rejecting the present, fat God incarnate was likewise what drove the papal party to their Mass canon and its sacrificing. They both altered the central promise of Christ given in the Lord's Supper by making the words into their own prayer of "thanksgiving."

Why did both Zwingli and the pope cover Christ's proclaimed promise of his body as forgiveness of sins by
prayers of their own making?

Zwingli initially seemed to be wary of the central verse
of John—"the Word became flesh"—because he believed
God couldn't change (especially into his opposite, a body).
So instead of "the Word became flesh," he read the sentence as a trope and reversed it: "The flesh became word."
He exchanged the subject and object of the sentence in
much the same way that Erasmus had tried with Pharaoh's
hardened heart. Zwingli thought reason itself would be
offended by God apparently becoming something he
wasn't before. What kind of a God changes into something
different, especially a body? Zwingli and his sacramentarian
followers didn't want Jesus to mean "This is my body" in
much the same way that Nestorius didn't want Mary to be
the mother of God. So they raised all sorts of "reasonable"
objections, such as that the notion was gross, it was papis-
tic, it pursued the flesh rather than the spirit, or simply that
Jesus couldn't be in two or more places at once—unless he
left his body sitting up in heaven with the Father and was
present here as "spirit" in the thoughts and memories of
people and in his divine nature. Zwingli then used the old
method of reading Scripture called *alleosis*, which applied
any offensive Bible verse to only one "nature" of Christ or
the other, without any communion of attributes. Anything
that is undignified for God was then referred to "the man"
Jesus; and anything that was too good for a human being
was given to "the divine" nature. Luther called that the
"damned *alleosis*," because underneath its use was the
attempt to protect oneself from the charge that a preacher
must make: In killing Christ you killed God.

Nevertheless, as Zwingli's type of reformation theology
took hold it began questioning the way Christ was given to

sinners, since Jesus once said, "The flesh is useless" (John 6:63). Did that not imply that body and material things cannot save but spiritual things such as fellowship or remembrance do? Since switching subject and object in the sentence "This is my body" did not seem to help much ("My body is this"), Zwingli tried another alternative: "This *represents* my body." Luther could hardly believe it, since this took the church right back to the first sin in the garden of Eden, where refusal of God's words and receiving God in the masks of created things first began the game of hide-and-seek for better (more spiritual) words. Body again became a sign or window to look through to get higher, spiritual things such as a peek at the naked God who hides behind good and evil. Consequently, dreams developed about how holy people mystically "participate" in God's spirit or are taken up to commune with the persons of the Trinity which led to the belief that you do not

really have to die in yourself if you accomplish certain legal requirements. Luther wanted to be rid of both those who sought to avoid the *crime* of killing God and those who wanted to avoid the *sentence* of death by carefully applying Scripture's words to a "safe" nature of God.

A light then went on for Luther. He sensed that Zwingli's new interpretation of the words "This is my body" worked very much like the old, Roman version of *transubstantiation*, in which a theory is offered about how bread actually becomes body and wine blood when the proper priest has momentarily opened the way for Christ to come back for sinners. This rational theory turned the Lord's Supper into a type of sacrifice, and the priests became a type of mediator for humans to connect to the divine. Both sacramentarians and the papal party assumed from the start that Christ was absent, then both altered Christ's words to fit a new theory about how to represent Christ (that is, get him to come back) and so connect the faithful to his redeeming work on the cross. They each did this by using words in the form of a prayer that helped the gathered "remember" what Christ had done—one by the canon of the Mass and the other with a series of prayers reminding the congregation of what Christ once did and what they were to do now in response (give thanks, or *eucharist*).

Luther had already concluded in his *Babylonian Captivity of the Church* (1520), that the papacy was guilty of falsely spiritualizing God's grace in an especially egregious fashion. Popes had authorized an ongoing evolution of what they considered God's mystery of sacrifice at the heart of all Christian worship in a prayer known as the canon of the Mass. Luther thought that act was not only the key to papal power but was also the very *anti-Christ*. The mass prayer came to be attached to the Lord's Supper and made Christ's promise of forgiveness into an act of *sacrifice to* God rather than a *gift from* God. It reversed God's direction and put humans together with Christ as if a saint and Christ were working in tandem for their own redemption. In part, the priest would ask God: "Grant that the sacrifice which I, though unworthy, have offered in the sight of Thy majesty may be acceptable to Thee and through Thy mercy be a propitiation for me and for all those for whom I have offered it up."

By authorizing this prayer, the pope was seen by Luther as a self-appointed preacher who substituted his own words in the form of a *prayer* for Christ's words that are a *proclamation.*

Luther believed both Roman liturgy and the sacramentarians substituted their own prayers for Christ's actual words of promise. Yet "This is my body" is not a ritual action that "spiritually" makes Christ present inside or outside the bread and wine. Those words, for Luther, do not *remind* people about a promise; they *give* it in much the same way that intercourse with a spouse *is* love rather than merely *represents* love. Then it dawned on Luther that both groups wanted an absent Jesus for a secret reason: to give themselves room for imaginary free will.

The lingering problem in the church, Luther saw, was Nestorian in nature. Jesus' incarnation for both groups was like a one-time break in the wall that stands between time and eternity, matter and spirit, infinite and finite, God and human. When Christ ascended into heaven in the sight of his disciples (Acts 1), he also supposedly took his body and blood. That seemed to create a gap in the electrical current between a would-be believer and the actual arrival of Christ, a gap the church had to fill by completing the circuit. When you do not have Luther's kind of "fat God" actually present in this old world, then the large gap

171

between God and humans can be filled only by the church, and its priests, or by decisions of a free will to accept Christ. For Rome, special ministers were ordained as successors to Peter and the disciples who were then considered "vicars" of Christ, or stand-ins, whose God-given power to make Christ present again in a "Eucharist" celebrates Jesus' re-presentation. The church then became a sacrament itself, and ministry became a stand-in between Christ's two natures that needed to be reconnected in mysterious rituals done by specially empowered priests of the cult. Neither Rome nor the sacramentarians wanted a Christ so fat in the world that one cannot help but bump into him because it left no room for them to be mediators.

The church, for Luther, was not a sacrament or collection of like-minded people trying to be spiritual; it was the sinners who are gathered around Christ because they have heard his promise that forgives sins. They have no other God than this particular man, who weighs so much because the sin of the world is upon him even in his body. Luckily, Luther thought, Christ is always here as head of the church and isn't going anywhere else. For Luther, God is not an "in and out" God but an "all the way God." If Luther was right, the long Nestorian intoxication and hangover in the church was about to come to an end.

Christ's Last Will and Testament

Consequently, Luther rejected the Supper as a sacrifice or a remembrance covenant and instead called it Christ's "new testament." He may well have come to this after reading the many commentaries that linked the priest and the canon of the Mass to the book of Hebrews, which describes how Israel's sacrifice and priesthood are presumably made new in Christ, but Luther believed that was a misreading of the book. The book of Hebrews specifically rules out offering sacrifices "day after day," since Christ is the one priest and his cross alone the sacrifice that ended all sacrifice "once and for all." Luther saw a mistake that ran throughout the church's theology of sacraments at this point. Baptism, the Lord's Supper, and absolution from sins were not extensions of earlier Old Testament promises given only to Jews (such as circumcision and Passover). To think that way about sacraments was to make a double mistake. On one side, it diminished the very promises made to the Jews by thinking that Christian churches had been given the correct or improved versions of these acts of worship. Thomas Aquinas was just following that custom when he called the sacraments "*new* laws" that evolved into higher forms with Christ and his church. On the other side, it misrepresented the promises of Christ as just another form of law. Consequently, there were endless discussions in the church about who is holy enough to give the sacraments and who is holy enough to receive them.

Luther began to teach that at the Lord's Supper, Christ was giving a promise. The promise took the specific form of a *testament,* as Hebrews puts it: "He is the mediator of a new testament, so that those who are called may receive the promised eternal inheritance, because a death has occurred that redeems them from the transgressions under the first [testament]" (Heb. 9:15). We still use this biblical language in everyday life when we refer to someone making "a last will and testament" for disposing his estate after he is dead. In making a will or testament there is first the testator (or will maker) who is anticipating her own death. The will itself is then drawn up and published so that it is legally recognized—often on a piece of paper with the proper legal language. There is also the naming of heirs and of the estate that is going to be left behind. That, Luther believed, is what Christ did at his Last Supper. It is a countercultural, odd, and even offensive last will to those who think they deserve something from Christ. If you have ever seen families fight over who gets what in someone's will, you get a sense of the problem. In the Lord's Supper, Jesus is the will maker who has the full power to name his heirs. The heirs he names are his very betrayers gathered around the table—even Peter would betray Jesus before the night was out and the cock crowed three times. That is why the publicizing of the will took place "in the night in which he was betrayed." Jesus knew people would question whether he was in his right mind in doing so, so Scripture refers to Jesus' careful attention to the preparations and the announcement of his own betrayal ahead of time. With the heirs named, Jesus then named his estate—"for the forgiveness of sins." That is a truly spiritual estate that is a new kingdom or world created as the opponent and definite end to "this sinful world." What that estate gives the heirs is forgiveness—no furniture or cars.

Luther reminded people that forgiveness of sins doesn't leave you back at square one to try harder on your next go at life; it is the very opening of heaven itself, and so eternal life permanently interrupts this old world with its own new world. To work properly, a will must take present, legal form in order to convey its promise. Normally that means a will is written on paper and signed with witnesses. Christ's will is not sealed by a signature on paper but is sealed by Christ's command that gives his promised forgiveness apart from the law in his own self: "Take; eat; this is my body which is given for you." Just as with a legal document, this promised freedom comes by the means of a physical, tangible "thing" that coincides with the estate actually given "for you." Taking and eating as Christ wished is the mask where God himself wants to be found and grasped in word and thing. Whenever Christ's last will and testament is declared publicly, it is going to be contested bitterly by all the powers of this world that seek to bind, accuse, and condemn you for your sin as measured by the law. That means this will must become a battleground where Satan, death, and your own sinful self will seek to prosecute their own rights against Christ's free gift. In light of that set of accusations, you would then need to produce proof of your right and just claim to Christ's kingdom of forgiveness. Satan and his horde will call you into question in one way or another: "This cannot be; you are a betrayer, unworthy, sinful, unclean," or they will use the opposite tactic: "You do not need this since you have your works to make you right, you have your 'faith' that you yourself have decided for, and so forth." Against these, one produces the evidence: "But I am in truth Christ's betrayer and have done as he commanded—taken and eaten, and so I am named in the will and his estate belongs to me."

At Christ's Last Supper, Luther noted, all was then ready for sinners to make their claims of the forgiveness of sins and eternal life—but for one thing. In order for the will to go into effect the will maker must die. What if the heirs colluded in his death? What if they gave him up, ran from him, or participated in the very death? Here Christ's unbreakable, unthwartable promise and will must hold against all the powers the old world has to muster—sin, death, and the devil—for Christ gave this estate to the very ones who needed it, namely, his betrayers. Only the sick need a physician. This addressed the question of how Christ's cross, which is a historic event of the past, nevertheless saves people who come later. The last will and testament is announced but only goes into effect at the death of the testator. All of the attempts to connect people ritually, mystically, or liturgically to Christ's once and for all sacrifice on the cross in the form of resacrificing or representing had to come to an end. The Lord's Supper was a publicly proclaimed word that works both law and gospel in the lives of sinners.

Here we also find Luther's solution to the continual problem in Christian theology of holding together both parts of Augustine's definition of a sacrament (word and sign). The will as paper is not the actual estate offered, but it does more than merely refer to it symbolically. The paper is more than a pointer to an absent thing or a spur for the memory of survivors; it is the thing you cling to and preserve so that when accusers challenge your right to the deceased's estate you produce the paper and say, "Here it

is, my estate, my promise, my right, and you cannot dispute it!" If you lose the paper and declare to your accuser, "I cannot find the will," this is more than misplacing the furniture of the estate. Your right is lost. Your justice according to the law is left unfulfilled. The consequences of not finding the paper will are equivalent to losing possession of the estate. The paper and the estate are identified as one for you, clung to as life itself. Likewise, the wine and bread, body and blood of Christ are received by faith as the undeniable right to chase out from the conscience any question of your forgiveness. Instead, they give you the right to let Christ sit in your conscience saying, "You are mine; I have claimed you."

For this reason, Luther refused the debilitating "improvements" to the words "This is my body" by both the papal prayers of the Eucharist (canon of the Mass) and the theories of symbols from the sacramentarians. Let Christ's words to his betrayers be proclaimed as the public reading of his will, Luther taught. By that proclamation

Christ bestows his whole spiritual kingdom on sinners in a little word of promise, his own body and blood hiding in the mask of bread and wine and given to be grasped and eaten.

So at the Marburg Colloquy in 1529 (a meeting called by political leaders to heal divisions between Luther and other reformers in their political defense against Rome), Luther refused to equivocate on the words "This is my body." From that point on, Lutherans would part company with a series of other reformers. Luther wished Zwingli well, but asserted that he had become "of another spirit" than the Holy Spirit.

When they are given Christ *alone* as the one who is right, neither the church nor the world wants "to give up its own righteousness," Luther noted. "Just as a monkey loves its own offspring, so the world loves only those things

which belong to it. . . . [A]ll other things which are outside itself and rest only on faith, it proudly neglects and treads on as though on an unknown treasure."[5] Luther was being very tough, of course, but as even his friend Melanchthon tepidly admitted, a bad disease requires a "harsh doctor," and apparently God had given one in Martin Luther. The entire world's virtue, especially its religious type that comes in acts of sacrifice, is finally only "monkey love" when it comes to God. But God has come down deep in the flesh to crawl through death to life in order that accomplished sinners might die under God's wrath. Then they are raised by his unthwartable mercy apart from the law in Christ. To have that fate, Luther thought, is what it means to be free.

CHAPTER ELEVEN

Freedom of a Christian

For freedom Christ has set us free.

(Galatians 5:1)

A "fat" God sunk down deep in world and flesh, the man Jesus Christ, produces "fat saints." The old, monastic idea of saints who sought to deny their bodily desires and transcend their world through spiritual exercise or to use others for their own merit ended with Luther. He believed that the exchange between Christ and his sinners takes all your sins and puts all his righteousness on you. The effect is to free you for a new life that is very much in the old world but not of it, a life that is like salt to preserve and provide taste to the creation and that, like leaven, fattens the whole loaf. Luther's insight was shockingly simple, as great ideas always are: God does not need your good works, but your neighbor does. That realization opened for Luther a new relationship that refused to make either creation or the law the means of salvation but to use them for helping others in need. God intends to manufacture good works through you for others, by hook or crook, because there are real people and things in the world that need your help.

Both faith and vocation are sheer gifts of the Holy Spirit instead of products of your free will cooperating with God's grace. Luther believed that "a good tree produces good fruit," but good fruit does not produce a good tree. The whole trick was getting the direction of things right. God is coming down so you can move out. This does not leave you to ask yourself how you can produce more fruit, but to ask how God makes you a good tree in the first place, apart from the law and in Christ. Before there is productive activity in your life for others there is complete passivity where God alone is doing what God does—creating new things. Then God's new creation is a truly living and active thing that "lives large" in the world as a means through which God preserves and enhances life.

Faith: Freedom and Slavery

If you do nothing for salvation and are perfectly passive before God, are you not then worthless, idle, and as good as dead? Hasn't Luther removed holiness, spirituality, and morality that rightfully should be the heart of religion itself and the motive for doing good works?

From both sides of his critics, Luther was seen as unspiritual. He broke the mold of religious types since, on one hand, he was the most enflamed sort of apocalyptic prophet and talked about the end of the world and the coming of a new kingdom with Christ, but on the other hand he was strangely too worldly. He was accused by his first slanderous biographer, Cochlaeus, of being too lusty because he liked playing his lute late at night. Luther was indeed very worldly since he believed the cosmic battle won in Christ's death and resurrection ended the constant attempts of sinners to run out of the world on quests for spiritual self-transcendence.

In his famous writing *The Freedom of a Christian* (1520), Luther admitted that his teaching broke the most basic rule of reason at the point where Christ permanently interrupts life with a promise. According to logic's basic law of noncontradiction, one thing cannot be wholly something and its opposite at the same time. But Luther recognized that two obviously contradictory things must be said about the new creatures that we loosely call "the Christians." For that reason, Luther's essay uses two theses not one, and they appear to be direct opposites:

> A Christian is a perfectly free lord of all, subject to none.
> A Christian is a perfectly dutiful servant of all, subject to all.[1]

The two sentences appear as direct contradictions, but we want to see if they in fact fit together much like when the apostle Paul described his own faith, "For though I am free with respect to all, I have made myself a slave to all" (1 Cor. 9:19). Free person and slave—how can both coexist in one person?

The first thing to consider in the theses is the exclusive

particles "none" and "all." Could Luther be any more excessive? Why all the absolutes? Faith means you are not just somewhat free but *perfectly* free. And you are not just a lord of something such as your own inner desires but *of all*, and you are not just subjected to some or one but *none*! This produces an entirely new way to think of yourself.

If you can only sing monotone and only know of your relationship to others and God as a form of law, then you can only think of yourself as a person who does good works or fails to do them. You *are* what you *do,* and so free will seems to be your real personal stuff. This is monotone and "skinny" thinking. Then faith alone becomes the most fearful deathblow to your spiritual aspirations, and death is counted as the end of your chances to improve by using your free will. Instead, Luther painted three dramatic pictures of what he called the "powers of faith" to fill in what looks like sheer nothingness to hide-and-seekers.

The first power of faith is to be free from the law.

When you cling to Christ's word of promise, good works mean nothing to God or to you. The only thing that matters between you and God is "the most holy Word of God. . . . '[I]f the Son makes you free, you will be free indeed'(John 8)."[2] Faith is absorbed, united, saturated, and intoxicated by God's word. Imagine that faith is like being drunk—losing one's own power and coming under the power of whatever God says.

The second power of faith means that not only is the conscience let out of prison, but it has been led to the very place where the *true* God wants to be grasped and held. The game of hide-and-seek is over once God's promises are honored. God has given himself to you in his words so that he is not just an invisible higher power but is graspable in his promise. That means that God is not hiding out of reach, but graspable and even *judged* by you as faithful or unfaithful to his promise. Your God has suddenly emerged from being an elusive fate, or mere chance, to become one whom you can recognize as being true, right, and gracious. Test for yourself—does God's word do what it promised to do? Did it make faith where you had none by your own fruitless seeking? The first commandment, and so all commandments, is completed by trusting that *God* is exactly right by making *you* right without works on account of Christ. Faith is not the start of something bigger yet to come; it is the arrival of life eternal all by itself. The true God has given himself to you in such a way that you actually trust him instead of waiting for the next shoe to drop. Luther was always amazed that he actually found the gracious God there in his promise, as given by the preacher, or bestowed in baptism, or eaten and drunk in the Lord's Supper. More accurately, as Paul himself once observed in the letter to Galatians, I did not find God, God found me (Gal. 4:9, au. trans.).

There is a third power that is then unleashed for faith. Paul called it boasting in the Lord. Luther called it asserting true doctrine. The word of God gives you the right to make fun of death: "Where, O death, is your victory? Where, O death, is your sting?" (1 Cor. 15:55). Having lived a little, you no doubt have learned the joys of scoffing, sarcasm, ridicule, mockery, and general contempt of what you hold to be beneath you. Nothing is finer than a beautifully constructed put-down of your enemy. Of course, we are taught not to overuse this kind of humor because it is very humiliating and destructive to be on the other side of it. It is also not humorous to be sarcastic about something or someone who has no power. But wouldn't it be great if once in your life you were able to scoff and mock at your greatest enemy without fear of reprisal? Wouldn't it be great to look into your own grave, like Dickens's Scrooge, and instead of pleading for more time just let go a great big laugh?

The third great power of faith shows itself when "the heart learns to scoff at death" without worrying about

reprisals later. This power is given because Christ's communication of attributes has extended to you through preaching. Think of a royal marriage having taken place between your soul and Christ, whose "wedding ring" is faith itself. In marriage, whatever the groom owned becomes the bride's at the moment the groom says, "I do." And when the bride says, "I do," all her belongings become the groom's. God has already taken the inventory of your estate and found three things: sin, death, and the devil's damnation. Going to the cross proves Christ was not fooled, after all; he really took what belongs to your soul—including his Father's own condemnation. Christ confessed these things as his own, at great cost, in order to defeat them in his own person. Yet to the contrary, what belongs to Christ? *Grace* that forgives sin, *life* newly raised from the dead, and *salvation* (eternal life). The trick for the soul is to learn how to apply its own things to Christ and Christ's things to it in what Luther calls "boasting." When you, the Christian, boast, it is not boasting in yourself but in Christ, precisely because his things have become your own through faith itself.

Simul: The Double Life

Undoubtedly the greatest problem with faith's boasting is that faith is *hidden* in the old world. What you *see* and what you *trust* are not the same; in fact, they are polar opposites in a bitter fight to the end. Consequently, faith must deal with a strange overlapping of the old that hangs on like "a bag of worms" and the new that mocks death. The gospel's hiddenness does not mean faith's powers are not there— quite to the contrary. Something that is *invisible* may not be there, such as a unicorn, but something that is *hidden* is definitely real and present even though it is overlooked by someone searching in the wrong place.

A person who stubbornly insists on being right with God by doing good works—even if helped by grace—just doesn't "see" faith. A person who looks inside herself for the divinity just doesn't notice a preacher who dispenses God's words. But the biggest problem for faith in God's words comes when people look at themselves as uninterrupted old sinners who cannot trust Christ's communication of attributes. The church has always struggled with the fact that people keep sinning after they convert or are baptized. But what does it mean that Christians remain sinners in themselves?

Luther placed all the authority with God's word to accomplish what it says—in baptism you have *already died*—and then he took the consequences of thinking this way. Before you could ever say with Paul that you are a "master" and "slave" at the same time, Luther concluded, you have to realize that you already have been made a sinner and a saint at the same time (sometimes called *simul* for simultaneously being two persons). There are two "you's" that do not "commune" but instead have an interrupting death that stands between them that is bigger than the Grand Canyon. When the preacher comes with God's words of law and gospel, it causes a rupture in your own person that will never be healed. From that point on you must think of your own "I" differently, with two absolutes that pertain at the same time: old and new, dead and alive, sinner and saint. Nothing made either the papal party or sacramentarians angrier at Luther than this insistence: After baptism not only does *sin* remain but the *whole sinner* is there—dead, helpless, passive, unable to do anything, and already divinely judged as having no future. If that were not bad enough, Luther understood that at the same time a *whole saint* is there as well, newly raised from the dead.

Identifying oneself in two absolutes simultaneously is of

course difficult and unnerving for our form of being or our "onto-logic." But more to the point for Luther, this distinction is fought against by the devil. He wants you to confuse old and new, Adam and Christ (Rom. 5), sinner and saint. He wants you to think of yourself as *partly* a sinner and *partly* a saint. Why? Because then you do not have Christ as the sole mediator. He wants you to think of having your own righteousness that is not infinitely dependent upon borrowing Christ's. He wants you to think of your life as gradually improving and then backsliding, and then

improving again in a kind of religious roller coaster of enthusiasm. Of course, the main instrument for confusion is to put the law in front of you and ask, "How are you doing, now that you are converted, saved, changed, became Christian, or whatever you think is so 'new'?" But Luther learned from Paul to speak directly to this charade, "But I am dead to you, law!"

Why is that so hard to grasp? Death is worse than you thought. It is not just ceasing to breathe and returning into the never-ending cycle of life and death; it is receiving God's *final judgment* here and now—before you are ready for it. In that case, your dreams of getting a good judgment from God at the last day, or being remembered forever for what you accomplished on earth, are revealed as frauds. It also means that new life (resurrection from the dead) is yours in a certain hope that is already accomplished *in faith itself*—but only there. Paul even says we "die daily," and Luther recognized in his *Small Catechism* that therein lies the enduring significance of baptism throughout your earthly life: "The old creature in us with all sins and evil desires is to be drowned and to die through daily contrition and repentance, and on the other hand that daily a new person is to come forth and rise up to live before God in righteousness and purity forever."[3]

Furthermore, your new life is alien. It is outside of the old "you." It is not a matter of Jesus coming and cleaning you out in order to use your old shell, or getting rid of everything but your little spark of free will. He comes to kill the old and make a new creation. This takes you away from the law as your self-identity. The first feeling that results is fear. Imagine the tragedy and comedy of a preacher coming upon someone bound and determined to cling to works and the law rather than Christ:

PREACHER: You have died.

SINGER: *(monotone)* Yes, but then what is my motivation in life?

PREACHER: The law is over.

SINGER: *(monotone)* Yes, but then how do I know if I'm getting better?

PREACHER: Christ died for you.

SINGER: *(monotone)* Yes, but what is my part? What do I do then?

PREACHER: You are no longer a slave but a free heir.

SINGER: *(monotone)* But what if I don't want to be a slave and lose my free will?

PREACHER: But you have died, remember? Christ is all in all.

SINGER: *(monotone)* But what if I don't want to die?

PREACHER: It's too late.

So Luther expounded on Galatians 2:19–20 to his erstwhile students (knowing that their jaws were dropping all the while):

> For those who scoff at Paul and say, "What are you saying, Paul? Are you dead? Then how is it that you are speaking and writing?" We respond, "There is a double life: my own, which is natural or animate; and an alien life, that of Christ in me. So far as my animate life is concerned, I am dead and am now living an alien life. I am not living as Paul now, for Paul is dead. Who, then, is living? The Christian. Christ is speaking, acting, and performing all actions in him; these belong not to the Paul-life but to the Christ-life.[4]

Luther's great lectures on the Sermon on the Mount assumed the same thing, that at every step you have a

"Paul-life" and a "Christ-life." You have a world-life (old) and a faith-life (new) that are whole and simultaneously overlapping for now, and each further than the East is from the West. You have an alien life wed to Christ that makes you right with God, and a native life that struggles to be right with other people according to God's law. So Luther concluded: "I do indeed live in the flesh; but this life that is being led within me, whatever it is, I do not regard as a life."[5] That simple assertion spells the end of metaphysics and ontology that postmodern philosophers have been searching for. Luther simply says, the old life—*whatever it is*. What was I before faith? Your guess is as good as mine. You appear now to have been a Narcissus, a navel-gazing theologian who was desperately curved in upon himself. But whatever I was, that is over now. The old life's clearest attribute was that everything and everybody dies in the end, and in the meantime this truth causes you and others to tell mythological stories to deny the truth, stories that

run all the way from reincarnation to suicide as the last act of pure freedom. But the Christ-life has become all *hope* and is the only "you" that has a future. So what if you cannot see it yet! You couldn't see what you looked like before you were born from your mother's womb either, yet that didn't stop you from being born.

Servant to All: A Good Tree Produces Good Fruit

The second part of Luther's *Freedom of a Christian* asks, What do I do now that I am already (prematurely it seems) made right by believing Christ's promise? Luther never changes directions or sets Christ aside to get to good works. He takes an illustration from Matthew 7:17 and says, now that you have been made "a good tree" (i.e., been made right with God), a "good tree produces good fruit." Out of faith comes love just as naturally as a good fig tree produces figs. Luther believed this was an announcement or assertion, not a motivational speech for the free will. It describes what God has promised to do with his sinners assembled by the word of the preacher.

Luther's description of freedom is the true opposite of a single self pursuing the goal of its own happiness. It is also the true opposite of the utopian dream of equal justice for all under the law. The free life is lived outside oneself in Christ, and all this by clinging to a bare, simple, and repeated promise such as that found in Scripture: "If the Son makes you free, you will be free indeed" (John 8:36). A truly free Lord of all becomes a servant to all freely, spontaneously, and naturally. Luther liked organic images, such as the good tree producing good fruit, because it is hard to go back to singing the law alone when you use them. Does the tree *have* to produce good fruit? What if the tree doesn't *want* to produce good fruit? Does it have

193

free will to say no? To faith, these questions now sound silly and "fruitless." Luther held that Scripture did the exact opposite of Aristotle's description of ethics. Good works do not make a person good, but a good person does good works.

Just as Christ put on the sinner for you, so you will "put on" your neighbor. In faith you do not live in your old self, as we have seen, but in Christ, and then in the works that God produces through you for your neighbor you once again do not live in yourself but come to live in others by helping them with their needs. You may begin to feel like you are being spread a little thin, but then again, when the object of life is not to become righteous by the law, giving yourself away doesn't seem like a loss but a gain. On this point, Luther was fond of quoting Jesus: "For those who want to save their life will lose it, and those who lose their life for my sake will save it" (Luke 9:24).

Holiness and Ordinary Life

For Luther, becoming a servant of all and a saint in this world opened up an entirely new way of life. Christians by Luther's day had traditionally distinguished "the religious" from all other Christians. Holiness, for example, had taken on the meaning of being set apart from others by denying bodily desires; refraining from sex in marriage was then better than having sex in marriage. Producing more monks rather than more children was considered a higher spiritual calling. Even Christ's Sermon on the Mount, which included such words as "turn the other cheek," was made into something the church called "counsels of perfection" that applied Jesus' words only to the highest form of saints pursuing an ascetic life.

Luther thought sinners routinely turn what God wants

for life upside down in this way. Later in Luther's life another group of "monkish" reformers called Anabaptists ("re-baptizers") believed that a Christian remained holy by refraining from holding public offices, refusing private property, and adopting pacifism as a higher Christian life. Such people refused any distinction between God's spiritual kingdom that comes from preaching and the old earthly or secular kingdom ruled by God's laws. Luther thought they confused God's two kinds of righteousness—one related to other people that did not concern salvation, and the other before God that alone made a person right. The common element in Roman or Anabaptist religious movements was separation from the world in order to become holier than the mass of humanity. The holiness, however, was based on made-up words that ended by directly opposing God's own words, such as "Be fruitful and multiply," and "Blessed are those who hunger and thirst for righteousness," and "Be subject to the governing authorities . . . the servant of God to execute wrath on the wrongdoer."

Instead of producing holiness at the extremities of life, Luther began to open up God's desire for what it was like to be holy in the *middle* of life. He became a great phenomenologist of earthly life, using God's law (the most salutary doctrine of life) to probe beneath contorted human inventions of false spirituality to find what God wanted normal life to be like. Marriage, having children, preaching, taking responsibility for the welfare of others, and resisting evil emerged as the kind of things humans are made to do in the middle of this life—not forming Christian communes or creating vows for higher forms of spiritual exercise in order to escape the world.

Luther began describing this life by observing that humans need things for living—from shoes on your feet to

a roof overhead and food for your body. Such things are usually provided to us by families organized around the relationship of parents and children. Parents are God's way of giving children the things they need. God actually promises these things to be given in more than ample supply when his law is done—parents loving children and children respecting parents. So a family is needed for a good life, which begins with a husband and wife procreating in a kind of cocreation with God that makes sexual intercourse a most holy matter. From this family, the economy of providing house, food, and shoes originates.

Luther thought God also provides for life by creating another "estate" called the ecclesiastical or churchly, by which God finds a way to tell people his will by *speaking* to them. The church, according to Luther, did not begin on Pentecost or at the Last Supper and is not confined to "Christians," but at creation itself God made the church by God giving words to Adam and Eve so they could worship him truly. There from the very beginning of the creatures' relationship to the Creator stands the preaching office. The first preacher was God himself, and the first sermon was simply: "You may freely eat from every tree of the garden; but of the tree of the knowledge of good and evil you shall not eat" (Gen. 2:16–17). The church is created by God's word. It stands under it as a creature. In it God makes an office for a preacher that is first given to Adam and Eve to hand on to their progeny.

God's ways of life that include family and church do not give over to the church a power to rule the family or vice versa. Luther began to see that you must refuse the claims of church to rule marriage and the government and you must refuse attempts of governments to rule the church. Eventually this became the rather one-sided notion of the separation of the church from meddling in the business of the state, but just as important is the need for the state to quit creating its own religion and forcing people to worship its false gods. Luther was teaching something historians call "two kingdoms," but really it is

just learning the proper place and use of the law and where that law must stop.

Most especially, Luther concluded that the office of the papacy had no place in any of God's created ways of life. It was a human imposition that showed its evil disposition by attempting to invade and control each of God's own created "estates": the church, the family, and the government. The office of the pope has nowhere to stand in God's ways of life, and therefore it began to protrude as a dangerous human tradition that contorts life by its endless legal pronouncements about its own power. At the same time, Luther was resisting the constant tendency of Christians to withdraw from the world because of its evil and so to create their own imaginary forms of holiness.

God's First Use of the Law after Sin

Unfortunately, Luther cannot say much more about God's word and true worship before sin, since humans proved to be bad at both families and church. Those two ways of life have been deeply embattled and wounded from the start. You know of Adam and Eve's sin. Cain, the first son of Adam and Eve, carried on their tradition by displeasing God in worship, and then proceeded to wreck the family by killing his brother and dishonoring his parents. Because of this trail of evil, God established a limit to evil and a power for good works to help neighbors by giving a government for the wider "family" of one's society. The apostle Paul described this authority as God's servant for good: "Let every person be subject to the governing authorities; for there is no authority except from God, and those authorities that exist have been instituted by God . . . for [the authority] is God's servant for good" (Rom. 13:1, 4). Luther was convinced that this governing authority was established on earth because humans became sinners in search of other words. They ruined the church and family and so God also established the essential, limited work of civil government, which uses reason and the power of "the sword" to limit evil in this old world. Luther extolled reason and human free will to exercise proper dominion in those created things given to its jurisdiction.

God sanctions and uses power in the form of parental, police, and military authority to make and enforce laws. This power, however, cannot eradicate violence itself, nor can it defeat the goal of violence—death—because it cannot overthrow the power of the devil or our own sinful selves. Confusion over the uses and limits of this power of the law especially makes church people swing between extremes of pacifism or anarchism. Often such people then create theories about the need to establish God's righteous kingdom on earth, perhaps even through violent rebellion!

The law describes life accurately, and whether it comes in the form of common sense descriptions about what we need to live in this life, or specific words written on stone tablets and given through Moses to his people in the wilderness, it tells us that we owe God fear, love, and trust. Moreover, we owe all three to God at the same time. Further yet, we owe love to friends and enemies alike.

How are you doing with this owing? The law is right and you must agree with it, but the law has a severe limit— it cannot *give to you* what it demands *from you*. It describes but does not provide; it demands but does not give. In the *Large Catechism,* the "teacher's manual" for Luther's *Small Catechism,* Luther noted that the demands "are set so high that all human ability is far too puny and weak to keep them."[6] If you are going to love your enemies and praise God for everything that comes your way in life, then you will need much more than a change in attitude or a

New Year's resolution. You will need a personality trans-plant—what the Bible calls a "new heart." In short, you need to be killed and made alive.

Vocations

Justified by faith on account of Christ means you suddenly have new *time* that is not taken up in hide-and-seek religion and you have new *space* or ways to actually help others that come through your "calling" in life. Once you have Christ in the conscience speaking words of comfort, then suddenly your "neighbor" (what is today called "the other") also is heard loudly and clearly. Your own "inner static" that obsessively contemplates whether helping another is good for you and God is finally silenced.

Then an even bigger picture of God's world opens. God has not been waiting for you to believe his Son before you can produce good works and acts of love for neighbors in need (including enemies). When the law is chased out of your conscience, it finally settles down to its proper place

"TO THANK AND PRAISE, SERVE AND OBEY HIM"

and work in your old "members," or external life with others—a veritable web of relationships that God uses to make you some earthly good.

God has been busy from the very first, manufacturing good works through you for others and limiting evil by using the law. Faith anticipates more and more how God has provided means to connect to others than ourselves even in the way he created things in the first place. No neighbor is nearer and more in need of you than a spouse, and so marriage of man and woman becomes the epitome of serving others as a sacrifice of oneself that is done freely, out of love—only to have oneself back in a new way. That does not mean becoming a doormat for abusers. Luther was speaking about the real *need* of others, not their *desire* for control or dominance or whatever desperate sin they use to reject God's word. God makes you useful for others according to his own purposes in the old creation by giving what Luther called "vocations," which call you out from your inner, self-protecting caves of hide-and-seek into the real world where others need you.

In a famous act of humanity, in the face of a peasant uprising and several capital punishments awaiting him from pope and emperor, Luther accepted a former nun's proposal of marriage (Katherine von Bora, whom he had helped escape from the convent in a herring barrel). He finally listened to God's word under all the clamor of the cosmic clash of spirits and the religious goals set for him by the monastery. That specific word from God had begun interrupting him years earlier just as he was about to become a monk. His father, Hans Luther, announced the command in Scripture to "be fruitful and multiply," but Luther resisted it, since in his religious quest he believed marriage and children were beneath him. But then his world turned upside down when Luther heard Christ's

word of forgiveness for all sin, and instead of trying to be more than human, he was free to become nothing more nor less than Martin Luther, teacher of the church, son of parents, husband of Katherine von Bora, and father of children. He was planted by God to make this created world his home and one that was hospitable to others. Suddenly Luther realized that life was not the pursuit of truth or piety or the mad game of hide-and-seek for better words. Life as God wanted it was about changing diapers when his child cried, giving lectures to strengthen his students, and preaching to comfort consciences troubled by the law and God's wrath. Getting married was not only what God approved for him, but it had the added benefit, Luther joked, of spiting the pope and bothering the bishops.

What better act of humanity could be committed—striking a blow for God's own new kingdom against the devil's raging—than his marriage? Luther began the remarkable turning of his life to the vocations of daily relations that please God: marriage, parenthood, teaching, preaching to a congregation, and fighting tirelessly in the church against enthusiasts of Roman or spiritualist bent. Practicing the art of distinguishing law and gospel, demand and promise, became the stuff of his letters, conversations with friends over dinner, lectures at the university, sermons, and words of advice called out by the struggles that constantly rise in church and society—because we are in the last death throes of this evil world and its evil prince. For in those little words, "Christ forgives your sin," we have and trust our Creator because he is "with us in the muck and work of our lives so much that his skin smokes." Therefore, Luther—*sinner* in himself, *conqueror* in Christ, and so *useful* to his neighbor—found the odd delight of Christian faith under the cross while this old world remained. He became truly spiritual and worldly at the same time—master of all, servant of all.

CHAPTER TWELVE

Fame and the Cross

Luther was the first nobody (not a king, messiah, general, or bishop) to have what we call fame. Partly he was famous due to the growing use of the printing press, which spread his writings far and wide in an instant. And Luther did write! Partly he was famous (or infamous) because the great powers of his day, an empire and the Vatican, made an outlaw of him and threatened to burn him at the stake. Mostly though, his fame came from his simple teachings of justification by faith alone and vocation for others, which still stir violent debate. In Luther's own words, he liked "to tell it like it is." He was determined to be what God called him to be—Martin Luther, teacher of the Bible and preacher of the same, husband and father, friend and child. It is at least instructive to see what happens when someone is as determined as Luther to fulfill an earthly calling as he understood God intended.

Fame is a double-edged sword. It made Luther the most reviled and hated person of his age, and at the same time he was beloved and revered by many even while upsetting deep-seated traditions and assumptions in both church and society. His enemies called him a seven-headed monster, among more unprintable things; friends called him a prophet, and beloved teacher. When his colleague at Wittenberg, Philipp Melanchthon, was told of Luther's death, he cried, "[O]ur charioteer has fallen . . . our Elijah—because he unleashed God's promise of justification by faith alone *that defeated death,* thereby refusing any other God than the man Jesus Christ."[1] Luther was what Christians once called a "confessor," a real sinner whose witness to Christ brought down on him the world's and the church's persecution. Luther lived and died having been excommunicated by the Roman pope and declared an outlaw of the Holy Roman Empire. All of this happened because he pointed relentlessly to the one thing he thought mattered about Bible, church and faith: *God is right in making God-haters into his beloved children because Jesus Christ died for their sakes.* That is what the Bible is all about, what Christian worship and service is about, and what life is about, Luther concluded. Why would such a simple teaching cause so much upset and violence in both church and world? In short, justification by faith alone takes away the most cherished and oft-told fantasy humans hold about themselves and God, and anyone who takes Christ seriously comes up against what Luther liked to call "the big death." Without trust in his words, God is really, infinitely angry. Yet in Christ, where there is a big, fat death, there is also a big, fat resurrection—by whose Holy Spirit you are made new, free, forgiven, beloved, and truly alive.

Luther was a man who always had Jesus Christ in his mouth. As pious as that may sound, he discovered what happened when you open your mouth and Christ's promise comes out—all hell breaks loose. In fact, no one is ever madder at Christ saving sinners apart from works required by the law than religious people. Just as the Pharisees were offended by Christ at every act of forgiveness apart from the law, so in Luther's day the defenders of religious law emanating from the throne of the pope in Rome believed Luther was "a wild boar" who had gotten loose in God's vineyard, rooting up and destroying good, Christian order in the church. The church decided early on that Luther had to be gotten rid of, but, as they say, the plans of mice and men oft go astray. To this day, churches and their people across the globe bear his name (Lutheran), as a result more of their detractors than their friends. Nevertheless, Luther was pleased to establish churches in his own day that did in fact refuse to be known by anything but the public confession of faith in Christ's promise of forgiveness as the only way that sinners are made right with God. They were known as Evangelical or gospel churches because they sang two notes, law and gospel, and not just one.

The insignificant German monk changed the world by

his little writings, lectures, and sermons, inaugurating what historians now simply call "the sixteenth-century Reformation." Yet what was more important to Luther himself was that he managed not just to change the course of history but to interrupt it permanently by throwing Christ's preached promise "for you" (while you are yet God's opponent!) into the middle of life. What followed were chaos and a beautiful new creation, God's own version of a wickedly comic sense of humor at the heart of life: "God chose what is foolish in the world to shame the wise; God chose what is weak in the world to shame the strong" (1 Cor. 1:27). That is the sum of Luther's life, ending in the same kind of declaration he found in Paul's letter to the Corinthians: "God is the source of your life in Christ Jesus, who became for us wisdom from God, and righteousness and sanctification and redemption, in order that, as it is written, 'Let the one who boasts, boast in the Lord'" (1 Cor. 1:30–31).

His last written words are often remembered to this day: "This is true, we are all beggars."[2] By the time Luther died, he and his fame were all used up. Nothing was left of him to boast in but his Lord, Jesus Christ. But at least for Luther, that was really something.

Notes

Introduction

1. "Luther at the Diet of Worms, 1521," in *Luther's Works: American Edition*, ed. Jaroslav Pelikan and Helmut Lehman, 55 vols. (St. Louis: Concordia Publishing House; Philadelphia: Fortress Press, 1958–1986), 32:112. Hereafter cited as LW.
2. "Ninety-Five Theses," in LW 31:25.
3. "The First Sermon, March 9, 1522, Invocavit Sunday," in LW 51:77.

1. In the Beginning . . . a Preacher

1. "Bondage of the Will," in LW 33:1.
2. "Small Catechism," in *The Book of Concord: The Confessions of the Evangelical Lutheran Church*, trans. and ed. Theodore G. Tappert (Philadelphia: Fortress Press, 1959), 345.

2. Law and Gospel

1. *Sermons of Martin Luther: The House Postils*, vol. 1, ed. Eugene F. A. Klug (Grand Rapids: Baker Books, 1996), 84.
2. Ibid., 86.
3. Ibid., 91.
4. Ibid., 87.
5. "Apology of the Augsburg Confession" IV:8, in *The Book of Concord: The Confessions of the Evangelical Lutheran Church*, ed. Robert Kolb and Timothy J. Wengert (Minneapolis: Fortress Press, 2000), 121.
6. For familiarity I will stay with the translation offered in the *Lutheran Book of Worship* (Minneapolis: Augsburg, 1978), no. 229, except where it departs too far from Luther's German text given in *Luthers Werke*, Kritische Gesamtausgabe,

ed. J. F. K. Knaake et al., 57 vols. (Welmar: Bohlau, 1883ff.), 35:456–57. Hereafter cited as *WA*.

3. Justification by Faith Alone

1. "Table Talks," in LW 54:442–43.
2. "The Preface to the Latin Writings," in LW 34:328.
3. Ibid.
4. "To Casper Mueller, November 24, 1534," in *Luther: Letters of Spiritual Counsel*, ed. and trans. Theodore G. Tappert (Philadelphia: Westminster Press, 1955), 39.
5. Aristotle, "Nicomachean Ethics," in *The Complete Works of Aristotle: The Revised Oxford Translation*, ed. Jonathan Barnes (Princeton, N. J.: Princeton University Press, 1984), 1783 (E, 1129b 28).
6. Immanuel Kant, *Critique of Practical Reason*, trans. L. W. Beck (Indianapolis: Bobbs-Merrill, 1956), 89.
7. Aristotle, "Rhetoric" in *The Complete Works of Aristotle*, 2174 (1366b 9–11).
8. "To Philipp Melanchthon, June 29, 1530," in *Luther: Letters of Spiritual Counsel*, 150.

5. For God, to Speak Is to Do

1. "The Keys, 1530," in LW 40:325.
2. "Psalm 2," in LW 12:33.
3. "Lectures on Galatians, 1535," in LW 26:153ff.
4. *The 1529 Holy Week and Easter Sermons of Dr. Martin Luther*, trans. Irving L. Sanberg (St. Louis: Concordia Academic Press, 1999), 139.
5. *Sermons of Martin Luther: The House Postils*, vol. 2, ed. Eugene F. A. Klug (Grand Rapids: Baker Books, 1996), 192 (translation altered by author).
6. "Smalcald Articles" III.iii.30–33, in *The Book of Concord*, 317.
7. "The Sacrament of Penance," in LW 35:17 (italics added).

6. What Theology Is About

1. "Psalm 51," in LW 12:310.

2. *Luther: Lectures on Romans*, ed. and trans. Wilhelm Pauck (Philadelphia: Westminster Press, 1961), 235–36 (italics added).
3. Ibid., 239.
4. Ibid (italics added).

7. Bound and Accused

1. "Psalm 51," in LW 12:307.
2. Ibid., 311.

8. God, Who Forgives Sin

1. "Lectures on Galatians, 1535," in LW 26:150.
2. *WA* 39/1.349f, translated in James Arne Nestingen, "The Catechism's *Simul*," *Word and World* 3, no. 4 (1983): 367.
3. *The 1529 Holy Week and Easter Sermons*, 119–27.
4. "The Freedom of a Christian, 1520," in LW 31:349.
5. "A Brief Instruction on What to Look for and Expect in the Gospels," in LW 35:118.
6. Ibid.
7. "Wittenberg Preaching Fragments 1515–1520," in *WA* 4:608.32–609.1.
8. "Lectures on Galatians," in LW 26:30.
9. "Chalcedonian Symbol," in *The Creeds of Christendom: With a History and Critical Notes*, 6th ed., vol. 2., ed. Philip Schaff (1931; repr., Grand Rapids: Baker Books, 1993), 62.
10. "Smalcald Articles" II.5, in *The Book of Concord*, 301.

9. At Great Cost

1. Anselm, "*Cur Deus Homo*," in *St. Anselm Basic Writings*, trans. S. N. Deane, 2nd ed. (La Salle, Ill.: Open Court Publishing Co., 1962), 246 (italics added).
2. "Lectures on Galatians, 1535," in LW 26:215.
3. "Defense of the Translation of the Psalms, 1531," in LW 35:216.
4. "Lectures on Galatians," in LW 26:278 (italics added).
5. Ibid.
6. Ibid., 281–82.

10. This Is My Body

1. "Smalcald Articles" III.iv, in *The Book of Concord*, 319.
2. "Concerning the Order of Public Worship," in LW 53:11.
3. "Lectures on Galatians, 1535", in LW 26:18.
4. "Confession concerning Christ's Supper, 1528," in LW 37:218.
5. "Psalm 2," in LW 12:19–20.

11. Freedom of a Christian

1. "The Freedom of a Christian," in LW 31:343.
2. Ibid., 345.
3. "Small Catechism," 349.
4. "Lectures on Galatians, 1535," in LW 26:170.
5. Ibid.
6. "Larger Catechism," in *The Book of Concord*, 431.

12. Fame and the Cross

1. Bretschneider, Carolus Gottlieb, and Henricus Ernestus Bindseil, eds. *Phlippi Melanchthonis Opera*, 28 vols. (Halle: C. A. Schwetschke, 1834–1860), 6:57–59.
2. *WA* 48:241–42.

For Further Reading

Luther's own writings

Luther's Works. American ed. Edited by Jaroslav Pelikan and Helmut Lehman. 55 vols. St. Louis: Concordia Publishing House; Philadelphia: Fortress Press, 1958–1986.

Luther's Works on CD-ROM. Minneapolis: Fortress Press; St. Louis: Concordia Publishing House, 2002.

Martin Luther: Selections from His Writings. Edited by John Dillenberger. Garden City, N.Y.: Doubleday, 1961.

Materials about Luther

Brecht, Martin. *Martin Luther.* 3 vols. Translated by James L. Schaaf. Minneapolis: Fortress Press, 1985–1993. These three volumes give a comprehensive biography of Luther.

Forde, Gerhard O. *On Being a Theologian of the Cross: Reflections on Luther's Heidelberg Disputation, 1518.* Grand Rapids: Wm. B. Eerdmans Publishing Co., 1997. This book introduces not only Luther's early breakthrough but also examines his enduring work of distinguishing cross and glory.

Junghans, Helmar. *Martin Luther—Exploring His Life and Times, 1483–1546.* Minneapolis: Fortress Press, 1998. This CD-ROM uses a variety of media to help understand Luther's times.

Kittelson, James M. *Luther the Reformer: The Story of the Man and His Career.* Minneapolis: Augsburg, 1986. This book is the best place to go for a short biography of Luther that stays true to his theological center.

Lazareth, William H. *Christians in Society: Luther, the Bible, and Social Ethics.* Minneapolis: Fortress Press, 2001. This is now the basic work in English on Luther's political and social teachings that concern God's two ways of ruling the world.

For Further Reading

Lohse, Berhard. *Martin Luther's Theology: Its Historical and Systematic Development*. Translated and edited by Roy A. Harrisville. Minneapolis: Fortress Press, 1999. This book is now the standard introduction to Luther's theology, laid out first in historical periods, then in major themes.

Lutheran Electronic Archive from Project Wittenberg. Translations of some of Luther's works can be found online at this address: www.meditatio.org/etext/luther/

Lutheran Quarterly (www.lutheranquarterly.com). This online portion of a journal dedicated to Luther's theology (and the church that bears his name) is a way of seeing how modern theologians convey and argue about Luther and his legacy.

McKim, Donald K., ed. *The Cambridge Companion to Martin Luther*. Cambridge: Cambridge University Press, 2003. This collection of essays is a great way to learn about Luther's theology in detail along with the current theologians, churches, and movements influenced by him.

Nestingen, James A., and Gerhard O. Forde. *Free to Be: A Handbook to Luther's Small Catechism*. Minneapolis: Augsburg, 1975. This is the most popular, recent teaching manual for Luther's single most important writing on God's word and the Christian life.

Index

215

Index

Index

217

Index

Index

Jesus Christ
  (continued)
  preaching of, 69,
    148, 161
  present, 171
  and Scripture,
    38–39
  the word or
    Logos, 79,
    133, 150
Jews. *See* Israel and
  the Jews
Job, 129
Joel, 17
John the Baptist or
  forerunner, 23,
  26, 83–84
John, 18, 23–29, 79,
  82, 133, 150,
  169, 185, 193
judge, 7, 9, 27, 39,
  42–46, 55–61,
  71–75, 79, 82, 95,
  114, 126, 149,
  159, 185, 188
justification by faith
  alone, 28–29, 36,
  37–52, 108, 138,
  156, 206–7

Kant, Immanuel, 42
keys. *See* forgiveness
kingdom of Christ, 9,
  18, 28, 41, 79,
  86, 141, 144,
  152, 159–65, 175,
  178, 183, 195,
  197, 199, 202

Large Catechism,
  94–96, 199
law, 7, 8, 36, 44, 65,
  149, 153, 167,
  170, 184, 190,
  192–93, 195–96,
  199
  accusation of, 83,
    121

apart from, 40,
  47–52, 162,
  179
before and after
  Christ, 128–31
cursed Christ,
  150–56
defined, 26,
  121–22
end of in Christ,
  62, 81, 127,
  129, 155
eternal or not, 85,
  127–30
as the form of
  grace, 74
as goal, 59–62
God's, 24, 136
as guide or
  teacher, 59–62,
  113
living beyond, 164
magnifying sin, 92
as original order,
  59
reducing the
  demand of,
  73–74
as self-identity,
  190
singling out the,
  31, 128
works of the, 7,
  11, 20, 22, 25,
  81, 84, 158
law and gospel, 17,
  38, 41, 50, 57–58,
  69, 72, 75, 81,
  120, 131, 137,
  154, 156–57, 163,
  165, 176, 188,
  203, 207
  confusion of, 58,
    65–66, 72, 75,
    81, 154
  distinguishing
    23–36, 69,
    156, 203

function of, 131,
  142
preaching, 120,
  137
Lecture on Romans, 60
*Lectures on Galatians,
  1534,* 151–60
Lectures on Genesis,
  106
letter and spirit,
  53–67
liturgical, 138, 171,
  176
logos. *See* Jesus
  Christ: the word
  or Logos
Lombard, Peter, 71
Lord's Supper, 22,
  139, 162–63,
  167–79, 185
love, 11, 54, 56–59,
  80–81, 92–103,
  106–7, 115,
  121–24, 129, 135,
  142, 151–54, 159,
  171, 178–79, 193,
  199–201, 206–7
  disordered, 117,
    121
  falling in, 95,
    98–100
  of God, 57, 80
  God's love of
    unlovely, 115
  of highest ideals,
    101
  imitation of
    Christ's, 151
  of neighbor, 38,
    45, 57
Luke, 64, 79, 194
Lutherans, 138, 167,
  207

Manicheism, 20, 150
Marburg Colloquy,
  178
Mark, 18, 148, 156

Index

marriage, 187,
194–95, 197,
201–2
Mary, 2, 138, 168
masks, 38, 79, 106,
160, 162, 169,
175, 178
Mass, 4–10, 164
canon of, 5, 167,
170, 173, 177
sacrifice of, 4, 8
Matthew, 86, 162,
193
means of grace. *See*
sacraments
Melanchthon, Philipp,
31, 50, 139, 179,
206
mercy, 62, 75, 110,
114–16, 121, 124,
137, 144, 149,
160, 171
merit, 20, 44, 49,
80–81, 181
*Mighty Fortress Is Our
God, A*, 34–36
monk, monastic, 5, 7,
8, 38, 41,108,
142, 181, 194,
201, 207
monkey, 178
monotone, 29–33,
115, 135, 154,
184, 191
moral, 20, 41, 50, 55,
64, 66, 81, 101,
112, 119, 128,
130, 149, 182
Moses, 27, 39, 46,
62, 65–66, 78, 82,
128, 130–32, 199
Muentzer, Thomas,
10, 11, 129
mystical, 5, 10, 20,
26, 30, 38, 54,
137, 164, 176

Narcissus, 95, 192

Nathan, 122
neighbor, 38, 57,
182, 194, 198,
200–3
Nestorius, 137–42,
167–68, 171,
173
new creation, 16,
18–19, 79, 159,
182–83, 190, 200,
208. *See also* old
and new: creation
new kingdom, 144,
159–60, 162, 165,
175, 183, 202
new Lord, 120, 141,
190
new person or crea-
ture, 83, 86, 141,
144, 183, 190
New Testament, 24,
28, 67, 128,
173–74
Nicea, council of, 136
Nietzsche, Friedrich,
50, 128
ninety-five theses, 8,
83
nominalists, 85

Occam, 38, 58
Oecolampadius, 139
office, 20, 195
of the keys, 70,
86. *See also* for-
giveness of sins
of preaching, 50,
164–65,
196–97
old and new, 19, 21,
33
creation, 79, 190
Adam or Eve, 86,
188–93
worlds, 21, 33,
35, 103,
148–49, 176,
182

*On the Councils and
the Church*,
138–45
On Translating, 158
ontological, 29–30,
36, 50, 60, 136
153, 189, 192
ordinary life, 194–98
ordination, 163–64.
See also call
Ovid, 110

pacifism, 195
pantheism, 105
parents and families,
2, 6, 96
honoring, 74–75,
196–99, 202
particula exclusiva,
158
passive, 22, 41, 160,
182, 188
passover, 173
pastoral care. *See*
souls: cure or care
of
Paul, 16, 25, 39–49,
53, 55–58, 62, 64,
81, 97–98, 107,
111, 119, 127,
133, 151, 153,
156, 158–61, 183,
185–88, 190–92,
198, 208
Peasant's War, 10, 40
129, 201
pelagians, 52
penance, penalty, 6, 8,
67, 69–74, 120,
151, 154
Pentecost, 196
perfection, 33, 81,
141, 194
1 Peter, 163
pharaoh, hardening of
heart, 112, 123,
168
Philippians, 47

221

Index

Philo, 54
philosophy, philosopher, 50–51, 76, 79, 91–92, 97, 106, 136, 140
pilgrimage, 4, 6
Plato, 15, 52, 60, 98, 118, 154
pope (papacy) 3–5, 8, 11, 50, 81, 121–22, 138, 164, 188, 202
　abomination of or no place for, 80, 198
　authority of, 66, 86
　and Mass canon 167–68, 170
prayer, 4–5, 7, 70, 75, 83, 138, 142, 164, 167–71, 177
　praying against oneself, 124–25
preaching or proclamation 7, 11, 37, 40–42, 47–50, 56, 60, 82–83, 86, 93, 95, 110–11, 115, 119, 120–22, 128–42, 148, 157–64, 168, 171, 185–97, 202, 206, 208
　announcing forgiveness, 115, 128
　application of the pronoun in, 55, 131–33
　and bondage, 119
　external and divine, 13–22
　office of, 138, 64–67, 195
　speaking for Christ, 136, 142

predestinating, 106, 113, 145, 160
Preface to the Latin Writings, The, 39–52
priest, priesthood, 4–9, 70–87, 135, 163–64, 170–72
　of all believers, 163
　as judge, 70–76, 80
　local forgiveness person, 86
　Mass priest, 164, 170–73
　as mediator, 83
　as a medical doctor, 69–76
　pastor, 69–87, 98, 165
　as proclaiming ambassador, 79
printing press, 205
progress, 1, 20, 22, 62, 90
promise, 2–3, 7–8, 11, 16–19, 21, 24, 27, 35–36, 48–66, 69–79, 84–86, 100, 106, 109, 116, 119, 120–24, 129, 135–36, 144, 157–59, 163–78, 183–85, 193, 196, 203, 206–8
　something to hang onto, 124, 185
Psalms, 34, 77–79, 91, 121–23, 158
purgatory, 5, 6, 8, 59

Quintillian, 53

reason, 3, 17, 24, 33, 44, 49–50, 52, 90, 115, 118, 128,

143–45, 168, 183, 199
rebellion, 11, 35, 57
reformation, 168, 208
relation, relational, relationship, 17, 31, 41, 48, 59, 64, 93, 96, 98, 101–2, 107, 115, 118, 154, 182, 184, 196, 201–2
religion, religious 30, 60, 105–8, 136, 145, 149, 163
renaissance, 3
repentance, 7–8, 70–76, 83–86, 120–22, 190
　God repenting one, 120–23
　and law, 81
　and signs of sorrow, 70
　true, 82–87
resurrection from the dead, 2, 15, 26, 50, 79, 82, 84–85, 130, 157–60, 187, 190, 207
rhetoric, 51, 53–54
righteousness, right relationship, 5, 9, 17, 19, 22, 26–28, 31, 37, 40, 59–69, 71, 79, 80–85, 115, 123, 130–31, 141–42, 147–49, 153–56, 162, 178, 181, 189, 190, 193–95, 199, 208
　Christ's own, 26, 47, 83, 85, 131, 181
　not in the self, 123, 153–54, 189

Index